Coping with Australia

Eleanor Greet

Basil Blackwell

Copyright © Eleanor Greet 1990

First published 1990

Basil Blackwell Ltd
108 Cowley Road, Oxford, OX4 1JF, UK

Basil Blackwell, Inc.
3 Cambridge Center
Cambridge, Massachusetts 02142, USA

British Library Cataloguing in Publication Data

A CIP catalogue record for this book is available from the British Library.

Library of Congress Cataloging in Publication Data
Greet, Eleanor.
    Coping with Australia / Eleanor Greet.
    p.   cm.
    ISBN 0-631-16377-8
    ISBN 0-631-16685-8 (pbk)
    1. Australia—Description and travel—1981—Guide-books.
I. Title.
DU95.G74   1990
919.404′63—dc20   89–29733 CIP

Typeset in 10 on 11½ pt Garamond
by Photo-graphics, Honiton, Devon
Printed in Great Britain by Billing and Sons Ltd, Worcester

Contents

Acknowledgements   vi

Getting acquainted: g'day   1

Getting the lingo: the language   4

Getting there: emigrating   9

Getting in and out of beds: accommodation   17

Getting around   23

Getting wise to money, phones, shopping and health   30

Getting down to food and wine   35

Getting into entertainment   45

Getting up a gum-tree: wildlife   51

Getting on with Australians   59

Getting bushed: the Aborigines   65

Queensland   71

New South Wales   80

Australian Capital Territory   85

Victoria   88

Tasmania   96

Northern Territory   106

South Australia   115

Western Australia   120

The Southern Cross   126

Useful addresses   128

Getting lost: Index   130

Getting found: Map   132

Acknowledgements

I have always been mindful of my great good fortune in being surrounded by warm and supportive family and friends, many of whom have contributed a great deal to this book.

It began with John Randle persuading me to write for people, not wastepaper baskets, a liberation which must be the literary equivalent of bra-burning.

As preparations for the Australian trip advanced, I became appalled by the expense, and was envisaging a semi-vagrant journey, sleeping on beaches and catching fish. Then on the point of departure my travelling companion, an old Finnish friend, the photographer Gledys Cloke, won a big prize on the premium bonds, which she immediately threw into the kitty – in this case the kangaroo's pouch. Remembering now that multicoloured journey, in all its facets of fun and wonderment, I cannot thank her enough.

What we did comparatively luxuriously, my son, Jasper Gerard-Sharp, did as a student in his 'gap' year, working his way round Australia in long coach journeys, wincing as kangaroos thudded and crunched beneath the wheels in the outback, and successfully rendezvousing with his friend, James Waters ('Meet you at the foot of Ayers Rock at dawn in three months' time . . .'). Shedding their English inhibitions, they slept in a tool shed with the spiders when the youth hostels were full, and saw the Great Barrier Reef for a fraction of the price it is for the not so young and hardy. I have Jasper to thank for trenchant observations on pub brawls, the seamier side of Kings Cross and how to avoid humiliation when surrounded by expert Aussie sportsmen, who ride horses, camels, surfboards and nasty horned cattle.

I am also indebted to Robbie Thorpe, an Aboriginal friend, for information not readily available, such as the burning, in 1940, of early Australian government records to obliterate from history the systematic genocide of the original inhabitants. Five billion dollars in ten years has been spent on Aboriginal affairs, most of it absorbed by a self-serving bureaucracy. The best information service is provided by the Koori Information Centre in Melbourne, run on a shoestring (tel. 03–419 9250).

There were many helpful research assistants, whom I would like to thank: my daughter, Lisa Gerard-Sharp, for plying me with press cuttings; Alison and Ian Ruff-Waters for varied comments on Australian life; Lorna Waters for encouragement as she read the first frail beginnings; Margaret Hunt for Aussie humour, as in the car stickers 'Live longer. Avenge yourself on your children' and 'Don't bugger the bush'; David Hunt for more erudite discussions on the economy; Hubert and D.J. East for excellent wine and food advice; Fiona Scott, Gill Walker and Geoffrey Bowers for Aussie colloquialisms; Chester and Zeny Cooke for outback information; Jennette Lavis for plays and new writing; Bevan and Barbara Scott for cartoons and scenic routes; David East for the expatriate viewpoint; Corinna Mowatt and Leslie Melville for background information; Ross Mowatt for being a spiritual Queenslander, almost a contradiction in terms; John and Rose Gittins for excellent cartoons from Western Australia; Peter Sawyer for political information; Dave Hodder for memorable tours; Don Hage for Northern Territory history; Jocelyn Maloney for outback humour; Diana Bryant for technical information on the wine industry; and a great Australian, Enid East, for just being herself.

I was forced into modern technology by a word processor, and had to call for help from Benita Dyal for demonstrations of its mysteries (just one more chapter, Benita?) and to Clare Treanor, who retrieved the Aboriginal chapter from limbo and saved me from my deadline. Thank you both.

In London the Australian High Commission proved an invaluable help, particularly Joe Rodigari, the Counsellor for Immigration, and Ken Steel in the press office. In Australia the tourist information centres cannot be praised highly enough. Whether the information is purely local or about another state, they have what you want to find, in a leaflet, on a computer or in their heads. Hotels and motels are equally helpful, taking tour bookings, arranging courtesy pick-ups and booking accommodation for you ahead. I would also like to thank all the information-givers at airports, bus stations and rail offices, who take all the tension out of travelling in Australia.

Getting acquainted: g'day

When it was first mooted that I should write *Coping with Australia* I quailed, because in my rebellious youth the only way I could cope with Australia was by leaving it.

At that time the country had a greater population of sheep than people, yet Australians herded themselves into small towns and cities of stifling gentility, fearful of what the neighbours might think – probably very little. There was a cultural barrenness to echo the deserts of the interior.

It was a White Australia of British stock, sadly depleted by two world wars, yet unmindful of the greater losses suffered by the Aboriginal people. To understand, you should remember that white Australians then were an island people descended from an older island people, whose inherited prejudices were reinforced by isolation in the southern hemisphere. Within that enclosed society, the term 'wowser' was coined to describe a mentality as narrow as a church door. A dissenter, I was squeezed out like toothpaste from a tube, and after university fled on the Great Escape route – a voyage on a P & O liner which took six long weeks to reach London, the farthest point in the world from Brisbane.

After living a longer time in Europe than I had in Australia, I returned as a visitor, hesitantly, but to my joy was given the proverbial prodigal's welcome by a warm, affectionate network of cousins and old friends.

This book is about what I found: a vibrant new image, a people to match a country of infinite variety. So many immigrants of different nationalities have changed the face of Australian cities, but, more importantly, changed the attitudes of the old guard.

Australia today

There is a new dynamism evident in a multicultural society. The Yartz, as all things cultural were once derisively known, have found form and voice through a growing national identity, so that Australian films, books, plays, ballet, music and painting are exciting to explore. With the debt to the Aboriginal people openly acknowledged, reparation is being made. They, too, have found a voice, and an international one at that.

With so much change, it was almost a relief to find that Ayers Rock was not festooned with neon lights, that I could still find my own oysters on Queensland rocks, walk for miles along deserted beaches and hear, with a new insight, the kookaburra's harsh bush laughter.

The people who had inherited my family home gave me one of my old schoolbooks and half a custard apple. The taste of the custard apple lived up to my memory of that exotic fruit, and free of all the past unhappiness I set off to explore my country.

Travel and tourism

For several months I swooped about by plane to cover the vast distances, and then from each chosen centre toured by car, camel, coach, boat, train and, best of all, on foot. Each state was memorable in its own individualistic way, each capital city encapsulating the character of its inhabitants; but in the hinterland behind the cities was the land I loved, still largely left to speak for itself. There has been a lot of philistinism in developing certain tourist attractions, but this is being curbed by a federal government determined to secure world heritage listing for threatened areas. Try to see as much of the country's natural grandeur as time and money dictate.

As a tourist, I encountered friendly, helpful people everywhere – the most outstanding being coach drivers/guides whose specialized knowledge was matched by good humour and genuine caring for the needs of their passengers. If you are enthusiastic and open, Aussies will respond; complain, and you are a whinging Pom/Yank/slaphead etc. On the whole you will meet the more interesting Australians in the least commercialized places. Cities breed a conformity of people as well as high-rise blocks.

Food and wine

Due to the multicultural influence on Australia since the 1960s, excellent food and wine is the norm, rather than the exception, and BYO (bring your own alcohol) restaurants are astonishingly cheap by European standards. The quality of the wine, fresh local seafood, vegetables and fruit is superb. When this is allied with sunlight sparkling on the sea many tourists glimpse what is often called the Australian dream, and plan to emigrate. If you do, I've written a totally boring, fact-filled chapter on how to set about it. The rest of the book is entertaining, the history cunningly concealed to unfold naturally in each chapter on the individual states and the Aborigines.

I intended to write a jolly chapter on 'Getting up to no good: sly grog joints and other no-nos', but the wine was so delicious I couldn't research evil wood alcohol, and gambling dens have largely disappeared, replaced by state-approved casinos, the nearest thing to a palace in Australia. In my youth, when alcohol was prohibited near a dance floor (I was brought up on 'Where there's Drink there's Danger'), I once had to sit with my feet in an ice-bucket of champagne concealed beneath the tablecloth while the police made their token, pre-warned raid, no doubt taking a drink in the kitchen while my feet froze. Like the Chinese opium den, the illicit drink-and-dance is a thing of the past, so I shall deliver no strictures.

The chapter headings are self-explanatory, dealing first with topics that apply to the whole country, from the language to the Aborigines, and then with the individual states and territories, moving from north to south and from east to west. All prices are in Australian dollars at 1989 levels, so allow for inevitable increases.

While I am writing this Australian g'day to you, it is a cold, grey day in London, and I yearn for the pungent scents of dry earth and eucalyptus trees, the warm seas and the nightly splendour of the Southern Cross. I hope you will come to love that strange country, where man and beast evolved in harmony with the land, undisturbed for so many centuries.

Although I never quite believed I would be, I'm really glad I never gave up my Australian passport.

Getting the lingo: the language

If you speak any form of rudimentary English you won't have many difficulties Down Under. Now don't come the raw prawn with me and complain you don't understand the tour guide. Just watch his lips. Alternatively, try following the yarn below, with the help of the glossary, and practise the lingo, preferably with a Fosters. An Aussie host is indoctrinating a Pom (Englishman) into the mysteries of a beach barbie (barbecue) with his mates and their sheilas (women).

A Strine yarn

'So the guide's lips don't move? No worries. *She'll be apples**, mate. Watch the sheilas instead. Any *fair dinkum* Aussie will tell you they're worth watching. Not talking to, mind. Keep over here with the rest of the blokes. We've just broken open another *sixpack of tinnies*. Beach barbies make a man thirsty. So you're a Pom, are you? I don't mind that. Some of my mates do, but I'm broad-minded. Get stuck into that *stubby*. Can't open it? Don't the Brits teach you anything over there? What d'yer mean "Apparently not"? You'd better *rattle your dags* and drink up or my mates will think you're a *one-pot screamer*.

Throw another steak on the barbie, Bruce. I could have played *footy* this *arvo*, but I went to a *buck's party* last night and I'm feeling a bit *crook*. I'll come good if that *drongo* doesn't eat his pie *within cooee* of me. Enough to make a man *chunder*, that pie – all those soupy green peas . . .

There was some *galah* last night *spitting his dummy* because his sheila had gone *beyond the rabbit-proof fence* with a *squatter*. *Out Woop Woop* way – she'll be back, my oath. Living in the back of beyond in

* For the meaning of words and phrases in italics see the glossary on p. 6.

some *humpy* with a *croweater* won't last. The flies
are something terrible. That sheila's a dead ringer for
Marilyn Monroe, so she'll be *up a gum tree* for
civilization. Can't see her lasting long, what with the
snakes and the outside *dunny*.

You don't know what a dunny is? Hey, this Pom's
a real *nong*. A dunny, cobber, is what the squatters
all use in the outback. It's a big, big hole in the
ground with a wooden seat on it and a *galvo* roof.
You pull your *strides* down and the flies come up to
get you, if a snake hasn't got you first. The squatters
chuck steak out for the *kookaburras*, to keep them
round the property, see? Yeah, that old *laughing
jackass* is your best mate *beyond the black stump*.
He watches from a tall gum tree, swoops down,
picks up the snake and drops him from a height until
he's dead – just so you've no worries on *walkabout*
to the dunny.

I was a *jackeroo* once, but couldn't see myself ever
owning my own *station* – joining the *squatocracy*.
Pity. Those squatters had it good in those days. My
oath yes. Money from the sheep's back made those
men kings. The bloke I worked for used to drive his
prize ram round in the back of his Rolls Royce.
Nothing too good for that ram. His missus used to
wear a mink coat at the Picnic Races, when all the
station people came from miles around and the bookies came up from Melbourne. Sweltering it was.
Ninety-nine in the shade, but she wanted to show
off her mink. A bonzer sheila she was. Put anyone
up for as long as they wanted. They were sleeping
all over the verandas and in tents for the Picnic Races
– hundreds of them – *flat out like lizards drinking* –
and she came out and said "Two spare beds on the
billiard table. Any players?"

The sheilas are ready with the *tucker* now. Then
we'll get our *togs* on and join the *surfies*. Another
stubby? No *wowsers* here, sport. Good on you.
You're not the *no-hoper* I thought you were. No
need to thank me. Next time it can be *your shout*.'

Glossary

arvo	afternoon
beyond the rabbit-proof fence, out Woop Woop way, back of beyond, beyond the black stump	the outback
bookies	bookmakers
buck's party	groom's farewell party
chunder	vomit
crook	ill
croweater	South Australian
dead ringer	spitting image
don't come the raw prawn with me	don't be obtuse
drongo, galah, nong	fool
dunny	outside earth closet
fair dinkum	genuine
flat out like lizards drinking	reclining at ease
footy	football
galvo	galvanized iron
humpy	originally an Aboriginal shelter; a shack
jackeroo	male station manager trainee (a female station manager trainee is a jilleroo)
kookaburra, laughing jackass	bird
no-hoper	useless person
one-pot screamer	person who can take only one drink
rattle your dags	hurry up (dags are heavy dirt-encrusted strands of wool on a sheep which make a rattling noise when the sheep hurries)
she'll be apples	everything will be all right

sixpack of tinnies	beer in six cans
spitting his dummy	having a temper tantrum
squatocracy	rich farmers
squatter	sheep farmer
station	farm
strides	trousers
stubby	short can of beer
surfies	people addicted to surfing
togs	swimming costume
tucker	food
up a gum tree	lost
walkabout	nomadic wandering
within cooee	quite near
wowsers	spoilsports
your shout	your turn to buy the drinks

If you followed this Strine yarn, you can laugh with the Aussies; but even so, don't expect to understand Sydney taxi-drivers. Fair dinkum Aussies often can't. Many new European and Asian immigrants end up behind the wheel of a taxi before they master the language, but they know Sydney well enough to get you to your destination.

You may be surprised by the use of 'unit' for an apartment or flat in Australia, and there is a potentially dangerous misunderstanding if asking for durex, which is the brand name for sellotape there. But on the whole it's simple. Aussies shorten everything, and put an 'o' or 'ee' at the end of the shortened word, as in touro (tourist) and footy (football).

Other expressions include:

as scarce as hen's teeth	nonexistent, they're so rare
be up a gum tree	be in difficulty
bring a plate	take pot luck
Buckley's chance	no chance at all
dob in	betray or inform
don't lean on the shovel	get on with the job

fossick (for gold or opals)	search for
get bushed	be lost, as in bush country
give the Aussie salute	brush flies away with the hand
go bush	go to the remote outback
have a bash	attempt something
have a go on the pokies	gamble on the poker machines
in the nuddy	naked
let a dingo (native dog)	destroy property
into the sheepyard	wilfully
make a blue	a mistake or argument
not worth a brass razoo	worthless
one sandwich short of a picnic	markedly unintelligent
put the bite on	ask to borrow
shoot through like a Bondi tram	go very fast
the way the mop flops	the way the cookie crumbles
when the cross turns over	never; because the Southern Cross is fixed in the starry firmament for ever

The coathanger is Sydney Harbour bridge, and the Land of Oz is Australia. If you are a tall poppy (high achiever), like the wise men of the east (Canberra politicians), be careful not to skite (boast). Above all, to get on well with Australians, don't be a whinger or a wowser. Enjoy yourself.

Getting there: emigrating

In the past two hundred years, Australia has become one of the greatest nations of immigrants, with only 2 per cent of its population representing the original inhabitants, the Aboriginal people. Everyone else is an immigrant or descended from immigrants.

The post-war years brought a great influx of Europeans who changed the predominantly British way of life considerably, but it was mainly in the 1970s, with the ending of the White Australia policy, that the foundations for a harmonious, multiracial society were laid. The economic and cultural advantages of a mixed society are now self-evident to the majority of Australians, the only debate being over the speed of migrant intake and the method of choice of those most likely to settle successfully.

Government immigration policies, generally considered liberal and forward thinking, were recently attacked by the Aboriginal Affairs minister, himself an Aborigine, for promoting Asian immigration too vigorously. He claimed that the cultural identity of Australia was at risk. Although there was a public outcry and the minister was severely reprimanded by the government for making a statement which was directly counter to government policy, it would be wrong not to admit that he expressed a view fairly prevalent among Australians of British stock, although not among Aboriginal people in general. Notwithstanding this, both the government and the opposition are firmly committed to a non-discriminatory global policy, with plans to double the migrant intake over the next five years.

As there are many more prospective migrants than Australia could possibly absorb, all the migration offices overseas are swamped with enquiries and

Immigration policy

applications, so I shall set out the various modes of entry to help you decide to which category you belong.

Modes of entry

The majority of intending immigrants need to have either a close relative, already established in Australia for a minimum of two years, who is prepared to act as a sponsor, or skills and abilities which will contribute to the economy.

Family Migration Scheme

Under the Family Migration Scheme, the sponsor must be a parent, husband, wife, child or fiancé(e) of the intending migrant, and must be prepared to vouch for accommodation and any financial assistance necessary to meet the relative's reasonable living needs for the first twelve months in Australia. In the case of elderly parents, the sponsor agrees to be financially responsible for ten years, or until they acquire Australian citizenship, generally after two or three years.

Concessional Migration Scheme

The Concessional Migration Scheme applies to brothers, sisters, non-dependent children, nephews or nieces, with the relative prepared to sponsor them on the same basis as that required under the Family Migration Scheme. Remember that the sponsor is legally bound to accept full financial responsibility, so that if the migrant is unable to find suitable employment, 'reasonable living needs' for up to twelve months could be a great burden on the sponsor.

Independent migrants

People with more distant relatives, or none at all, can apply as Independent migrants. In the Independent and Concessional category, as well as in the Family Migration Scheme, a selection process based on a points system is operated, to ensure that those granted a visa will have a good chance of settling quickly and happily soon after arrival in Australia. It is an objective system, with emphasis on employability, age, education and work skills.

There is a fairly comprehensive list of occupations, reviewed each year, ranging from that of an economist to that of a hairdresser, for which there are optimum employment opportunities. The prospective migrant scores points for employability from this range, judged on education, skills, previous work experience and employment arranged by a sponsor; points are deducted for a need for English-language or other employment training.

The age of the applicant at the time of the assessment interview overseas must be under 45, with maximum points given to the 20–34 age group. Additional concessionary points are given to those sponsored, the highest being for brothers, sisters and non-dependent children, with a lower score for nieces, nephews and those sponsored by an Australian citizen not related to the intending migrant.

The government aims for self-sufficiency in key labour markets, and so encourages skilled prospective migrants to apply under two complementary schemes – the Occupational Shares System (OSS), and the Employer Nomination Scheme (ENS), for which the points system does not apply. All principal applicants must be under 45.

Skilled migrants

Occupational Shares System Entry under OSS is highly competitive, with a specific number of jobs to be filled within specific occupations. These range through the professions and the trades, from electronic and industrial engineers, who must hold a relevant university degree, to skilled waiters or upholsterers. Professional people should have three to five years' postgraduate professional experience, and people with trades must have had formal training in their own country entitling them to recognized trade status, as well as a period of at least five years' combined training and employment experience.

The list of occupations is updated regularly, while special arrangements are made for varying new projected shortfalls, such as those in the metal and printing trades. You can obtain the list and application form at your nearest Australian overseas migration office. There is a fee payable when you lodge your application, which is not refundable if you are not successful, so check you have a skill listed on the OSS schedule, have qualifications which are recognized, are of good health and character and under 45. If you are allocated a share in OSS you will attend a migrant selection interview to discuss settlement prospects and will have to pass a medical check. The whole process will take several months, so make no final arrangements until you are advised in writing that you have been approved as a migrant.

Employer Nomination Scheme   This is designed to help the economy expand rapidly by encouraging Australian employers to attract skilled migrants to fill vacancies which cannot be filled from the local labour market. The government aims to establish ENS as the direct route for skilled migrants, with OSS as a subsidiary. After the employer and prospective candidate agree terms, the processing for ENS should be completed in a month. Help yourself by answering advertisements in Australian papers and writing canvassing letters to potential employers in your field, as well as applying for the current list of vacancies at your nearest migration office.

Business Migration Programme   People considered under the Business Migration Programme must intend to settle permanently in Australia and are required to furnish proof of their financial standing. This must be sufficient to establish a business and provide support for their family. They must also demonstrate an experienced and successful business background and be prepared to outline their plans for a business venture in Australia which will benefit the economy. Advice and assistance will be given at your migration office.

Other groups   Other groups of intending migrants eligible for entry include those over the age of 55 without close relatives in Australia, who wish to spend their final working years and retirement there. Proof must be furnished of transferable assets sufficient to provide a home and reasonable support services in the future. Changes to the pension system now allow pensioners to earn up to $1000 (see 'Getting wise to money, phones, shopping and health') twice a year over a short period for casual work, without deductions. Tax is to be imposed on a new range of investments, however, such as insurance and friendly society bonds, approved deposit accounts and deferred interest debentures, so take advice on the most equitable form of investment for you.

Provision is made for a special category of former Australian citizens and those who spent their formative years there and have maintained ties with Australia. Assessment is likely to be sympathetic.

People in a class of their own, such as those with a record of achievement in creative or sporting fields, and distinguished people of outstanding ability who would clearly represent a gain for Australia, could expect the head-hunting treatment. At the sadder end of the scale, there is always provision, according to the numbers that Australia can absorb, for refugees, displaced persons and others seeking a new start away from war-ravaged countries.

More than three and a half million people have migrated to Australia over the past thirty-five years, and the vast majority have not only adapted to their new environment, but have enriched it. Australians are often accused of being racists, but on the whole they are a generous, good-humoured people, their bark being worse than their bite.

What to take

Once you have been accepted as a migrant and done as much as you can to arrange future employment and accommodation, your next step must be to decide what to take with you. Shipping your goods, though expensive, is worthwhile if they are of good quality, because the cost of starting from scratch would be enormous, just at the time when you need to conserve your financial resources, and also because you will feel more at home in a new country with familiar possessions around you.

The only items not to take are wardrobes, PVC-covered sofas and chairs, television sets, refrigerators and cookers, whether electric or gas. The heat in most parts of Australia makes all plastic surfaces most uncomfortable to sit on, and Australian refrigerators have extra, fan-assisted power. All houses and units (flats or apartments) in Australia are supplied with built-in wardrobes, a refrigerator and a gas or electric cooker. All your other electrical items will work perfectly well as soon as you change the plugs to the Australian three-point type – different from the British three-point ones.

Should you take a car, cycles, garden tools, sports gear or Wellingtons, make sure they are completely clean of dirt, to satisfy quarantine regulations. No plants, cuttings or seeds are allowed into the country either, but you can look forward to magnificent tropical plants instead.

Shipping your goods

If you plan to take only a small number of goods you might want to save money by packing them yourself, and having the shipping company collect and deliver them and advise on documentation. Self-packed items are difficult to insure, however, and there are lots of problems concerning the complicated shipping documents, storage in your own country and in Australia, itemizing and valuing for insurance purposes, customs and quarantine etc. In fact, as a door-to-door operation, by way of the high seas, it is best left to the experts.

So whether you plan to take your complete house contents, your car and animals, or simply excess baggage which can be packed in a few crates, ask four reputable overseas shipping agents for estimates. Many removal firms are members of the Association of International Removers. Whichever country you are emigrating from, make sure you choose a specialist in overseas removals, that you have full comprehensive insurance and that arrangements are made in advance for your goods to be forwarded to your new address by an Australian removal firm. All competent international removers should advise you, do all the packing and documentation for you and make the necessary arrangements for their Australian contractor to deliver your goods safely. Give your contact address in Australia to the removal firm and get the name of their representative in Australia, with whom you must keep in contact after arrival, because

Your moving check list

- Confirm the removal date
- Prepare an inventory for Customs
- Prepare a valuation for insurance
- Supply a contact number for when you leave the house
- Supply your new overseas address and an address before you move to your new home
- Dispose of goods not going abroad
- Obtain invoices for car and new purchases
- Check on resident permits, import permits
- Check passports are valid
- Agree on comprehensive insurance
- Check regulations for pets
- Ask for an electricity and gas final account
- Cancel all rental agreements
- Tell your solicitor, bank manager and doctor
- Cancel the telephone
- Notify your insurance company
- Cancel subscriptions of magazines, clubs etc.
- Obtain medical certificate
- Check marriage and birth certificates
- Cash in remaining car tax
- Obtain car log book
- Fulfil outstanding HP agreements
- Arrange for mail to be forwarded
- Pay comprehensive insurance premium
- Cancel newspapers, pay milk bill
- Arrange for someone to look after children during the removal
- Arrange banking facilities in your new country
- Arrange for mains services to be disconnected
- Check your travel arrangements
- Personal items separated to travel with you
- Food in the house
- Confirmation of time of arrival
- Fitted carpets loosened
- All mains services disconnected
- Passports
- Vaccination certificates
- List of unaccompanied baggage
- Keys of trunks, cases etc.
- All necessary receipts
- Spare cash for your journey
- Addresses of friends, relatives etc.
- Address of your contractor's agent

List supplied by the British Association of Removers (BAR)

shipping is a long business; you might be in Australia for two or three months before your household goods finally arrive on your doorstep.

The comprehensive checklist shown was compiled by the British Association of Removers for their overseas specialist removers. It will ensure you don't forget anything vital, or even merely desirable, as in 'Arrange for someone to look after children during the removal.' Consult it early. Otherwise, at the last minute, a passport may be found to be out of date or keys may be lost. I heard of one family who turned up at the airport at departure time with their cat in a shopping bag, convinced he could sit on their laps all the way to Australia.

Getting in and out of beds: accommodation

From the visitor's point of view, the word 'hotel' in Australia needs to be redefined. It covers a range of accommodation, or lack of it, from the Regent Hotel in Sydney, voted by international business people as one of the top three in the world, to crude drinking establishments with beds on verandas conspicuously occupied. Provision of accommodation, however theoretical, is incorporated in the licensing laws, so the designation 'hotel' should be clarified before you leap into bed.

There are many five-star and medium-priced good hotels in all the large cities and at the major tourist centres, with remarkable new complexes being built at present as new playgrounds for rich international tourists. Sadly, there seem to be no planning laws to prevent insensitive building in areas of great natural beauty, destroying the very beauty that visitors are coming to see. Queensland is the worst offender: I flew over one complex being built literally on the Reef, rising grotesquely like a great white shark from the deep blue-green of the Pacific. On the Gold Coast, the beaches were once banked with towering sand dunes scattered with wild flowers; now their grandeur has been bulldozed and replaced by a wall-to-wall carpeting of disparately designed hotels which hide the beauty of the coastline. Unless this ugly building is banished to the hinterland, further destruction of Queensland's incomparable coastline is inevitable.

The better type of modern hotel is equipped with every comfort, including a pool, jacuzzi, sauna and good service, such as booking tours, cashing travellers cheques and providing prompt medical services if required. The more luxurious, and expensive, such as the Hamilton Island complex, include a Japanese translation service, baggage collection from the plane and delivery to your suite, a welcoming hostess to explain the extensive facilities (for instance, a full programme of entertainment changed daily with the towels) and a fountain playing while you shop for designer resort clothes in the hotel boutique. Sportive dolphins have a pool to themselves while visitors swim a slow circuit of an island bar, pausing to slip onto an underwater bar stool from time to time.

Older hotels Some of the old, colonial-style hotels, with wide shady verandas and beautiful wrought iron, are now being saved from demolition and refurbished. Depending on the management, they can be a delight, with whirring tropical fans instead of the ubiquitous air conditioning, and friendly service and good food.
There are also, off the beaten track, rather flyblown dining rooms and baking bedrooms. Do not venture into this range unless you have a recommendation from the local tourist board, or from one of the travelling sales representatives who will be found at the best middle-range hotels and motels, prepared to chart the best watering holes in an entire state.

Motels For the majority of tourists travelling on a medium budget, there are very good motels, often included as part of a package tour. Their standards are always adequate and occasionally exotic, such as one in the middle of Kakadu National Park, in the Northern Territory, set in verdant tropical gardens to afford the maximum privacy and peace, with a tame baby water buffalo and kangaroo gambolling near a swimming pool and jacuzzi, and an aquarium in the dining room. Even the most basic, such as those near an airport, provide twin-bedded accommodation with bathroom, always with an excellent shower, tea and coffee-making facilities, air conditioning, television and radio alarm, telephone and refrigerator. The refrigerator is a good hospitality indicator. You can open the door on an Aladdin's cave of goodies – champagne, wine and lager, fruit juices and melon – or the minimal jug of iced water (alarmingly yellow in Adelaide, but it comes out of the tap that colour there).

Some motels have self-catering facilities, a dining room and a swimming pool. Breakfast is often delivered to the room at an inclusive charge and guests are asked to tick their preferences from a list supplied the night before. There are no hidden extras and tipping is not required. You are expected to carry your own baggage, but in the smaller motels you park your car outside your door. In larger ones, there can be a long haul up several flights and along walkways, tedious if it's 35 °C and humid, as in Darwin, so it's advisable to keep a small flight bag packed with essentials for the overnight stop. With practice, you learn to pack enough for a four-day tour in a bag this size, and begin to wonder why you brought a variety of smart clothes you don't wear.

Telephone calls are monitored, but an honour system trusts guests to pay for what they have consumed from a well-stocked refrigerator. I was glad to learn that this trust is seldom abused, because at the end of a long day's driving it's marvellous to find a welcoming, cool, amber nectar, sport.

The honour system

There are several chains of motels across the continent which offer bonuses or discounts and book you ahead. Flag Inns, Travelodge and Homestead all maintain good standards, though variable within each chain. If the weather is hot, make sure there is a swimming pool. The motel and medium range hotel chains have similar prices (see under Booking and prices), ranging from $54 to $200 for two people per night (see 'Getting wise to money, phones, shopping and health'), depending more on the location than the standard of accommodation. Sydney, the Gold Coast and Barrier Reef are the most expensive locations, with Perth, Darwin and outback accommodation being roughly half their price. A 2.5 per cent tax is added to accommodation at Ayers Rock and Alice Springs.

Motel chains

An interesting alternative to the motel chains is provided by Colonial accommodation, in houses old by Australian standards – pre-1901 vintage – registered by the National Trust. They vary to such a degree,

Colonial accommodation

according to the character of the owner as well as the house, that it is not possible to categorize them, but as a slice of Australian life they are marvellous.

One of the earliest stone houses in Tasmania built by convict labour is not only interesting historically, but alive with the warmth of a farming family who look after guests as if they were friends. There are also boarding-house type establishments, cheerless as their cornflakes, and subject to individual restrictions such as 'We like to bolt the front door early' – the sub-text being 'Anyone abroad after ten is up to no good.' At one of the Colonial stays, delightful in daylight but a deathtrap at night, I was told 'If you want a light in the hall between your bedroom and the bathroom, there isn't one, but I suppose I could leave a lantern.'

With advance warning, an evening meal can be provided, either formally or joining in with the family. It is often called 'tea' and tends to be at an earlier hour than one might expect, so arrive before six. Prices are on a par with motels and lists and descriptions are available from the relevant state tourist centres. Make sure you have the location pinpointed on a good touring map, because some of the more interesting ones are on very minor roads.

Farms If you like the idea of getting to know the people and tasting life in the outback, try a Farm Stay. With farmers now facing a difficult time financially, more are turning to tourism to replace lost income, so you will find a great variety of Farm Stay properties, especially in the eastern states of Queensland, New South Wales and Victoria. You can travel by car, coach, rail or plane, either for a few days or several weeks, joining in a muster, feeding the calves, or going for a bush walk and a swim in a river or pool. Prices in this category vary from camp site rates to those of moderate hotels.

Accommodation varies from the spartan, in shearers' quarters, caravans and tents, to a luxurious cottage or staying in the farmhouse itself. Be careful to note the different terms in descriptions of farms. A grazier runs a sheep or cattle station (Oz for farm – see 'Getting the lingo: the language') on an enormous acreage, which is ideal if you are keen on horse-riding, while the owner of a mainly arable property is called a farmer, often colloquially the 'boss cocky'. If you farm in Britain, the costs of your trip can be offset against income tax, while you visit local saleyards and inspect top sheep, horse or dog studs.

Some of the farms are places of great natural beauty, or near national parks. Some are only a few hours' drive from Melbourne or Sydney, while others, in the real outback, although only a few hours by plane, may be several days by road.

Farm Stay booklets are provided by the state tourist centres with details of packages and tariffs, varying from $18 to $150 per day or a very reasonable top scale of $200 per week, for a memorable experience.

Youth hostels

For young people travelling about Australia there are youth hostels in every large town and tourist resort. We have to thank Backpackers, started originally in Sydney, for its first perception of the need for safe, cheap, clean accommodation for adventurous young people travelling light. Both Backpackers and the government-run youth hostels are very reasonably priced, approximately $10 per person per night, with dormitories and self-catering and recreational facilities ranging from merely adequate to almost sybaritic. Just as important as accommodation, however, is the companionable social life, so that friendships are made across the international board and jolly groups do a few weeks' casual labour, such as fruit picking, to pay for the next stage of the journey. See p. 129 for the addresses of two youth hostels.

Camping

There are numerous camp sites dotted about the country. Some, such as those in the Cape York Peninsula, can be reached by plane, sometimes as part of a package; others are on farms more easily reached by road. In many camp sites either tents or caravans are provided, but there are still places where you can pitch your own tent; for instance, on small islands in the Barrier Reef, after asking permission from the rangers' office or national parks office, details of which will be furnished by the tourist bureau in Townsville or Cairns. It can be lonely. A tourist boat calls with supplies, and the ranger checks that all is well, but I heard of one young European who couldn't wait to be taken off again after spending just one night alone on a tiny deserted island, imagining he heard a wolf howling. It is better to camp with a friend, because although the places are often idyllic, there are insect pests, sunburn and food preparation which need to be shared with humour.

House exchanges

There is a house exchange scheme operating in Western Australia, similar to other well-known ones operating between Europe and America. They take about six months to process and can be contacted through the Perth tourist information centre.

Booking and prices

If you have a month or longer in Australia, you can afford to play it by ear to some extent, booking reservations along the way. If you have only a fortnight, stick to two centres at the most, leaving your choice of excellent day trips to be decided after you have talked to local people.

Depending on location, premier range hotels such as a Sheraton, Regent or Hilton and prestigious resorts such as Hamilton Island range from $155 to $295 for a room for two people per night.

Medium range hotels are $65 to $115 for two people per night and the budget range of hotels is between $54 and $65 for two people per night.

Self-catering accommodation has the most extraordinary range according to the number of people and the location, from premier prices in Sydney and Melbourne, down to log cabins or tents in the outback, which are very basic indeed.

All tourist offices will furnish lists of accommodation within your price range, as will airline travel centres, available at every airport. For addresses of state tourist offices see p. 128.

Getting around

On arrival in Australia you will have to face a trolley hunt and baggage retrieval and probably long queues to go through the formalities of passport, customs and immigration control. You will feel travel-stained, disorientated, fuming and, indeed, fumigated – the last of these happens to everyone before they get off the plane. The worst is over.

An airport coach or bus will take you to the city terminal and often makes various hotel drops as well, so ask first if your hotel is convenient for the driver. If not, taxis on a rank outside are comparatively cheap by European and American standards, and air conditioned. Ask for an estimated price – Australian taxi-drivers are generally praised, like London policemen in days of yore, for their fund of information and for their honesty. You may be surprised to find that they wear shorts, prefer the passenger to sit in front, and consistently refuse tips.

On your first day, apart from staying awake, do as little as possible, and have an early Australian bedtime to recover from jet lag. If you start in Sydney, go to Circular Quay and board a ferry which gives an extensive harbour cruise with an interesting commentary. In the other capital cities, I suggest a half-day sightseeing tour of the city, by bus, again with a good guided commentary. In the larger cities one ticket entitles you to get off at various stops and rejoin the bus and the tour at a later time. In smaller towns, the tour bus driver gets out at stops to give you a running commentary, always informative and often amusing.

Tourist information centres are universally good. I was amazed by the friendly efficiency shown at a really small information booth on Flinders Street railway station in Melbourne. Single-handed, a man dispensed information on where to go and what to see in the locality and further afield, as well as on train difficulties and how to rescue someone's lost grandmother.

According to the expert information-givers, the main trap for the tourist is in attempting to cover too much ground in a comparatively short holiday, with a camera click of a crocodile here and a fairy penguin there, thousands of kilometres apart. You cannot see the Barrier Reef, for instance, in a weekend from Sydney. Even with domestic flights, the distances between the main tourist centres are vast. Decide on an area and then on transport and travelling time.

Prices Australian airlines, railways, coach and cruise companies and car-hire firms all offer their own distinctive form of getting around, often with comprehensive package deals which are excellent value. Prices in Australia for hotels, tours and cruises are seasonal, and the heaviest advance booking occurs in the Australian school holidays. These are different in each state and each year, but generally they are: mid-December through the whole of January, the hottest time of the year; about ten days in early April; and three weeks in June–July and the same in September–October.

By air Australians use planes casually and frequently – they have special ones for flying doctors, for herding cattle and for shark spotting. So it's not surprising that their domestic airlines carry you for a short hop or a long walkabout with speed and efficiency, yet with a casual air.

For internal air flights in Australia (strikes permitting) the two major companies (see p. 129 for the address of both), Australian Air Lines (government owned) and Ansett (privately owned), have identical fare structures. Together they cover most of Australia. For all people with an international return air ticket to Australia, not travelling by first or business class, there is a 25 per cent discount on the normal economy class internal travel. All journeys must be completed within sixty days of arrival and both passport and international ticket should be presented. Prices are charged according to distance travelled – for instance, Sydney to Cairns, 1970 km, is $283 (see 'Getting wise to money, phones, shopping and health'), Sydney to Adelaide, 1166 km, is $200 and Adelaide to Alice Springs, 1316 km, is $217.

Check-in time is twenty minutes or half an hour at the most before take-off, no smoking is allowed and service is impeccable. I travelled extensively with Ansett, paying my own fare as just another tourist, and found their booking offices in Australia invaluable for up-to-date information on the most interesting itinerary, and for booking tours, accommodation and flights on smaller airlines where necessary.

East West Airlines links Perth with the eastern coast, and also gives a large discount on fares purchased outside the country – 30 per cent.

Booking

Most of the smaller airlines can be booked through Ansett or Australian Airlines (AA), the only exceptions being those offering a single inclusive tour. If you are making a flight between major cities, investigate the fare structure, because discounts can be as high as 45 per cent.

When booking domestic flights in Australia, always take with you your passport and international ticket, and remember to request a special diet, such as a vegetarian one, if required. You never know your luck: I was once presented with curried beans for breakfast.

Accommodation service

An independent service at many airports is a display panel of hotels and motels. This gives a photo of the place, services and tariff. It covers every price range, and there is a free, direct phone call to the one of your choice.

By train

Compared with flight, travelling by train in Australia keeps its slow and peaceful rhythm in tune with the long stretches of warm, burnt grass and grey eucalyptus. Sometimes you cannot imagine arriving anywhere, but suddenly there is a town, like Alice.

There are no railways in the 'Top End' of the Northern Territory or in Tasmania, but you can travel by train from Perth, in that odd little left-hand corner, all the way round the coast to Cairns in the northeast, as well as making inland forays.

The price of rail journeys varies according to the standard of accommodation as well as the distance travelled. For instance, Sydney to Adelaide is $275 for a first class sleeper inclusive of meals, $208 for an economy sleeper inclusive of meals and $85 for an economy seat exclusive of meals. An economy seat from Sydney to Brisbane is $79. An Austrail Pass allows unlimited travel on the main-line rail systems, with prices from $520 for fourteen days (first class) and $320 for a budget pass for the same time, which does not include a sleeping car. Remember that sitting up for twenty-four hours in a crowded compartment is only marginally more comfortable than doing it by camel, so when planning long train journeys take into account the length of time taken as well as the price.

The most popular and most expensive train, the Indian Pacific, glamorous as one of the last few great train journeys of the world, links Perth with Sydney. It quickly leaves the fertile southwest corner to cross the Nullarbor Plain, an Aboriginal name meaning literally no trees; no nothing, in fact, until the rich and varied lands of three states begin to roll beyond your window. This train should be booked well in advance, as should all major journeys, especially if a sleeper is required. There are many interesting, cheap day trips by train which need no advance booking, including some on steam trains, chuffing and whistling at yesterday.

By coach   There is an extensive coach network covering most of Australia. Coaches offer the least expensive form of travel, yet one of the most rewarding, allowing you to design your own holiday. Again, study the distances, because of the time in-involved. The cheapest outback route is Adelaide – Alice Springs – north Queensland, memorable, indeed, before you relax in Townsville or Cairns.

There are three main coach companies for long journeys, as well as a multitude of small regional ones which offer excellent day trips, with commentaries. Ansett, Greyhound and Deluxe all offer a discounted price for 'go anywhere' tickets if purchased outside Australia. Your travel agent can arrange this. Two-to three-week tours with major and minor operators are competitive, so explore your options, making sure you know what kind of accommodation is offered, and whether you will be given enough time to explore the areas of your choice. Some whizz through the country too quickly for you to savour it.

By car

In a scenic area, a few days' car hire can be a joy. You can stop for a swim and a picnic, seeing the country off the beaten track. Hiring a car is simple, whether you book it through an airline offering a discount, or in any place that appeals to you. Remember to have your international driving licence and your passport with you, and take advantage of special offers such as accommodation vouchers, good touring maps and advice on local traffic laws and the availability of petrol in your touring area.

Driving conditions

Driving is on the left-hand side and cars are air conditioned. Major roads and even secondary ones are in excellent condition as part of the bicentennial drive to attract tourists, but there are hazards. Lane

(Reproduced by kind permission of Sean Leahy and Gerard Piper, © Columbia Features Inc 1989.)

discipline seems poor to those used to European motorway driving, and you will pass myriads of sad, squashed wallabies and other marsupials, so drive with care, and never at night in the outback – the animals are nocturnal and are mesmerized by lights.

The leading car-hire companies are Avis, Hertz, Thrifty and Budget, with prices ranging from approximately $45 a day to $67. The speed limit is 60 km in towns and 100 km in country areas, except where dangerous conditions or wildlife warnings are displayed. It is compulsory for all passengers to wear seat belts and for third party insurance to be added to every car-hire booking. Expeditions to the centre must never be undertaken alone, or you might never return. A four-wheel drive vehicle can be hired, but you must travel as part of an organized convoy.

By water and other means   Getting around Australia is not complete without trying the waters. There are long or short cruises of a truly exotic nature available, centred on north Queensland, under sail or motorized, or gently

'Don't worry about me! Get in there quick, and turn off the meter!'
(Reproduced by kind permission of Douglas E. Tainsh)

drifting, gazing through a glass bottom at the wonders
of the Barrier Reef. In South Australia you can cruise
for 800 km on a paddle steamer, or when you're in
Sydney spend the day with the river postman on his
Hawkesbury River round. If you tour Tasmania by
car or coach, consider cruising there from Melbourne
on an Abel Tasman liner. It is a short holiday in
itself, reasonably priced despite its elegant luxury.

You can also tour in the centre and the northwest
by a motorized desert vehicle or by that ship of the
desert, the camel; there are hot air balloons and rafts
on white water and cruises with crocodiles on
nodding terms.

So you're not a millionaire? Surprise me. Neither
am I. I am giving you all the options, but if your
budget is limited, and your holiday is for two weeks,
I would advise you to travel extensively by coach.
Sydney–Brisbane or Sydney–Melbourne, for
instance, cost about $40 as opposed to a flight of
about $200. At an affordable price, north Queensland
and the outback are accessible. Coach prices have to
be worked out carefully, as there are large discounts
available if you use the network extensively. For
instance, an Aussie wanderer ticket, valid for twelve
months, will take you all over Australia for $846,
while a seven day koala pass is $217 and a single
journey from Adelaide to Alice Springs is $135.
Tourist offices make coach bookings for you, and
advise on coach tours which include accommodation,
often the cheapest way to cover long distances.

Another inexpensive way of getting as much variety
as possible is to divide your holiday between the city
of your arrival and a Farm Stay, where you join in
with outback activities. Prices are in the 'Farms'
section of 'Getting in and out of beds: accommodation' and addresses are in 'Useful addresses'. And
don't forget that Sydney or Cairns, without exciting
day trips, are marvellous holidays on their own.

**Budget
travel**

Getting wise to money, phones, shopping and health

The things you take for granted at home are often the most difficult abroad – from money to health.

Money If you are planning a visit of six months or longer, open a bank account in Australia with one of the larger banks, such as the Commonwealth or Westpac. If you are going for a shorter visit, change your currency into travellers cheques in Australian dollars. You will find banks are open at international airport terminals to meet all incoming flights.

Currency Decimal currency is based on the dollar ($A), consisting of 100 cents. The somewhat lurid notes are in denominations of $2, $5, $10, $20, $50 and $100, while the coins are the bronze 1 cent and 2 cents, and the cupronickel 5, 10, 20 and 50 cent pieces. The aluminium-bronze $1 coin has irregular milling to enable blind people to distinguish it easily.

Cheques and credit cards You will probably find it convenient to use travellers cheques directly as ordinary currency, with proof of identity, in hotels and larger shops without having to cash them first at a bank. Cheque books are not often flourished, but the major credit cards (American Express, Master Card, Eurocard, Visa and Carte Blanche) will do nicely except in small country towns.

Banking Banking in Australia is friendly and courteous, with drive-in banks an added luxury. Even if you haven't got much money, this service makes you feel as if you have. Opening times are uniform across the country – 9.30 a.m. to 4.00 p.m. from Monday to Thursday, and 9.30 a.m. to 5.00 p.m. on Friday.

If the dollar is down you might consider investing in *Nuggets* gold bullion coins, now legal tender, though I shouldn't try presenting any at the local supermarket. Recreating the country's colourful goldmining history, the Australian Nugget is available as four coins, either as the 1986 First Proof issue (very limited) or as the mass-produced later issues (much cheaper). Each coin has a nominal face value of $100, $50, $25 or $15, though the actual value will always be based on the prevailing price of gold and demand for the coins. Expected to overtake the krugerrand on international markets, the Australian Nugget can be bought at banks throughout Australia as a full set, half set or individual coins.

A nugget is, in goldmining terms, a waterworn piece of gold, and four famous ones are depicted in the series. The most recent is the 'Hand of Faith', found with a gold detector in 1980 near Wedderburn, Victoria, in the golden triangle area. As it weighed 20.4 kg and is valued at $1 million, you might rather invest in your own gold detector and go prospecting.

There is no limit to the currency you can bring into *Currency* the country, but in case you find a nugget or win *regulations* one of the state lotteries, you are not allowed to leave Australia with more than $5000 in Australian currency.

For all emergencies, police, fire or ambulance, dial **Telephones** 000 (free call).

You will find grey STD telephones are conveniently *Direct calls* placed outside post offices and in all busy centres. They devour 20 c and 50 c coins, which drop down automatically as your time is used up. A time-band system of charges gives the cheapest time for STD calls from 6.00 p.m. to 9.00 p.m. Monday to Saturday, and from 8.00 a.m. to 9.00 p.m. on Sunday.

At city general post offices and airports the STD phones also offer ISD (International Subscriber Dialling). The code for overseas is 0011, and the charges are $1.50 per minute to the South Pacific, and $2.10 per minute to anywhere else in the world.

There are red phones, for local calls only, in bars, shops and hotels, which give you an unlimited amount of time for 20 c.

Telegrams and trunk calls

Telegrams and cables can be sent either by phone or by calling at a post office, but you should remember that post offices are closed at the weekends (except for small ones inside a store for stamps only) and open from Monday to Friday 9.00 a.m. to 5.00 p.m.

If you go through an operator for a trunk call, do not be disconcerted by being told 'It's in the choob' (that is, 'tube'), which loosely translates as 'Please hold.' Your number might be a party line in the outback – sharing not only a phone line but your conversation as well.

Shopping

Ironically, although Australia is very commercially minded, there is a limited variety of goods and products to buy. In the major cities innumerable shopping complexes have been built to resemble multistorey car-parks, totally impersonal and housing identical goods. The service, however, is friendly and efficient, including that in small corner stores or roadside market stalls. On the whole, expect food and drink shopping to be of superb quality and cheap, and clothes shopping of quality to be expensive.

What to look for

As a visitor, the goods to look for are all the sheepskin products, especially baby fleeces and ones for sick people to lie on. There is a special springiness in the merino fleece which is superior to any other.

Beautiful hand-embroidered tablecloths, mats, handkerchiefs etc. are worth seeking out, as are woollen goods such as sweaters (called jumpers) and travelling rugs. Wide-fitting shoes are available everywhere and so are colourful, well-designed summer clothes.

Distinctively Australian are opals, jewellery made from shells or gum nuts, Huon pine wooden articles, toys such as koala bears and kangaroos (made of kangaroo fur), souvenir T-shirts, and bush hats in leather or felt. Aboriginal arts and crafts vary from the exquisite to the tawdry, whether it's a painting or a boomerang. Please don't buy coral, as it encourages the unscrupulous to ravage the Reef, which is, after all, composed of living organisms.

Buy Australian wine, especially champagne at $4 a bottle, from bottle shops, often drive-in ones, and take it to a BYO (bring your own) restaurant. The quality of the wines is equal to that of anywhere in the world, yet they are still absurdly cheap.

Shopping hours are generally 9.00 a.m. to 5.00 p.m. or 5.30 p.m. Monday to Friday, and 9.00 a.m. until noon on Saturday. You will find some small businesses which stay open until late – not just those for food and drink, but occasionally even an enterprising bookshop.

Times and measurements

Australia uses the metric system of weights and measures, and temperature is in degrees Celsius. Electrical appliances from overseas need to be adapted for 220–50 volts and a 50 cycles AC three-pin plug – quite different from the British three-pin plug. Only leading hotels have outlets for 110 volts. I found the international adaptor was very reluctant to shake down the requisite three pins, and after numerous skirmishes abandoned it altogether. With hindsight, I would not have given an extensive holiday to an ungrateful adaptor, a hairdryer and a travelling iron.

Health

Australia is justifiably proud of its high standard of medical services, but professional expertise is expensive. You cannot afford to be uninsured. When buying your international air ticket, also take out a fully comprehensive health insurance policy, covering accidents and all health risks, to run inclusive of your departure and return dates.

People emigrating should apply to join Medicare, the Australian national health insurance scheme, as soon as they arrive, because there is generally a three-month waiting period before claims will be met.

There is a growing emphasis on preventive medicine and community care, with education programming to promote a healthy lifestyle. You will notice that a nation of sunlovers now wear hats, barrier creams, and T-shirts over swimming costumes; they have been made aware that the penalty for over-exposure to the sun is skin cancer.

Despite vast unpopulated areas in Australia, no traveller in the outback lacks for medical assistance in an emergency. There is an excellent flying doctor service operating twenty-four hours a day, which whisks patients off to hospital very speedily.

Chemists   If you need to have a prescription made up, there are some twenty-four-hour chemists, but the pharmacist is unable to dispense from a prescription made out by an overseas doctor unless it has been endorsed by an Australian doctor. You can bring into the country four weeks' supply of any prescribed medication.

Getting down to food and wine

If you are adventurous enough to eat fat, white witchetty grubs still wriggling on the end of a stick, you will have cause to be grateful. In a parched desert they are priceless liquid refreshment, though the heads are a little crunchy. Whether you are eating grubs from the roots of a witchetty bush because that's where the camel took you, or dining at a top Sydney restaurant on Rock oysters, also recommended alive, alive-o, you will find that the most salient feature of Australian cuisine is the superb quality and freshness of its natural ingredients.

Food

Don't be alarmed. Not all Australian recipes begin with Mrs Beeton's instructions for kangaroo tail stew – 'First catch your kangaroo . . .' You are unlikely to be offered boiled trumpeter and parrot pie or even jugged wallaby nowadays, though certainly buffalo steaks are popular with visitors to the Northern Territory, and only the name is unfortunate for Moreton Bay bugs, a delicately flavoured, tiny lobster in Brisbane.

The choice in food and drink is as varied and colourful as the land and sea which give it to you. On Aboriginal guided tours in remote parts of the outback you will learn a little about food gathering – good bush tucker – but don't expect to catch an emu or a scrub turkey after just one lesson. Start with something easy, and stationary. The traveller's palm tree, which spreads its leaves like a fan from east to west, conveniently serves not only as a compass, but as a life-giving reservoir. When an incision is made in the trunk a torrent of magically pure water gushes forth. Wild fruits, such as passionfruit and a small, dark plum, provide more vitamin C than the cultivated varieties, and are easy to find once you know where to look.

Food gathering

Your own food gathering, however, should not go unsupervised. In a Queensland rainforest we were each given such a small portion of a juicy nut that we quickly garnered more, only to be warned of dire consequences if we ate them. Half an hour later our Aboriginal guide pointed to a secret scoffer in our midst, or rather, disappearing rapidly and frequently into the bushes. Apparently the nuts had strong laxative properties . . . I enjoyed the sweet-sharp taste of wild honey and aromatic tea, but couldn't say that charred bandicoot was the flavour of the year.

On an uninhabited island you can safely gather your own oysters, catch your own Reef fish, and cook it on the beach while the sun goes down, the smell of wood smoke permeating the eucalyptus and tea leaves sprinkled onto a billy can of boiling water. Your meal takes longer than sitting in a restaurant, but the peace and beauty are as wide as the sky.

Take-away
food

More often than not, however, travellers on short holidays want to catch fast food, already packaged. In Australia there are many excellent alternatives to the 'ratburger' international chains, often in unexpected places. In Tasmania, for instance, we arrived at Hobart's international airport, two happy beachcombers still sandy and salty after an exhilarating scamper along Seven Mile Beach, hungry enough to brave one of those airport snacks that are infamous in Europe. To our delight, a Hobart airport prepacked sandwich consisted of delicious dark rye bread simply bulging with fresh salad and salmon.

The standard of bread generally is high, from the bushman's damper, an unleavened bread cooked over an open fire, to full-grained 'health' loaves and the traditional goodies from enterprising Swiss, German or French bakeries. Close your eyes as a croissant melts in your mouth and you're in Paris; open them, and Sydney Harbour is sparkling before you.

Healthy take-away foods abound in every capital city, often from tiny premises, operated by a rich ethnic mixture of Asian and European entrepreneurs, as well as the indigenous Australian. A seafood take-away is not just fish and chips, but can include crab, prawns or squid, oysters or mussels; and Italian or Thai take-away is similarly imaginative, with the vegetarian well catered for.

At some stage of your journey, do try the traditional Aussie take-away, a steak pie – preferably without mushy peas, which turn it into a 'floater'. I can recommend the lightness of its pastry and the good quality of its beef filling. Wayside stalls practically give away melons, pineapples, citrus fruit, avocados, bananas and salad crops, while even in the cities fruit and vegetables are not expensive, and are of superlative quality. Most motels have self-catering facilities, so that a combination of selective take-aways and local fresh produce make very good value-for-money family holidays.

Since the 1960s a steady flow of immigrants intent on opening their own ethnic restaurants has produced a veritable A–Z of exotic cuisines. Melbourne, a Mecca for 'foodies', boasts restaurants from Armenian to Zulu, with every nationality in between; almost as wide a range is in Sydney, and at least Italian, Greek, Thai, Chinese, French and Lebanese are in other capital cities.

Styles of cookery

With all these exotic national cuisines abounding, what, you may well wonder, is now typically Australian? You have probably seen TV commercials with Paul Hogan exhorting a mate to 'throw another shrimp on the barbie'. Barbecues are indeed part of the Aussie out-of-doors way of life, and almost anything succulent is thrown on the barbie, whether it is on a municipal site or in a private garden, and much fun is had by all.

There is still 'British' food in abundance, in restaurants and private homes, but 'typical' Australian food can no longer be classified as 'best of British' or even 'worst of British'. Each successive wave of Asian and European immigrants has had its effect on the national palate, so that a dish once uniquely French, or Italian, or Thai, or Chinese, has either been retained in its full character or absorbed in part, incorporated into the everyday menus of Australian bistros and restaurants. The quality of their fresh

produce is so superb that the simplest preparation
often makes a memorable meal, but a strong Asian
influence appears in interesting and unexpected con-
trasts of tropical fruits, spices and herbs with meats
and seafoods, as well as a visual display to delight
the eye. After a morning snorkelling on the Reef, a
typical buffet lunch on board the launch is laid on a
bed of palm leaves, with branches of brilliant tropical
flowers between avocados and shellfish, cascading
salads and melons cradling berries and passionfruit.

In the wine-growing areas the European influence
is stronger; the steak that once used to be
accompanied by fried onions or two eggs is now
partnered by snails in garlic butter and herbs; tagliat-
elle appears with oysters and scallops in salmon roe
sauce; avocado with crayfish; prawns with honey
and mustard. Cross-fertilization of cooking cultures
creates unique dishes in each restaurant, so that one
can trace, for instance, the Japanese influence on a
French dish cooked by an Australian chef. In the
Victorian wine districts venison, pheasant, goose and
free-ranging guinea fowl, as well as beef, lamb and
pork, are provided by local farms, as are the delicious
vegetables, so that a wine-tasting tour is also a gas-
tronomic event. Haute cuisine in Victoria is very
haute indeed: the soup of the day for a simple counter
lunch turned out to be cream of walnut with prawn
quenelles. Long live Victoria.

Seafood   In other states I found the best food was invariably
the seafood, whether shelled or finned, often at moderate prices. This seemed to be the consensus of
opinion among well-travelled tourists of many different nationalities (Americans, Japanese and Scandina-
vians in particular), some saying it was the finest in
the world. Praised internationally are Sydney Rock
oysters, Tasmanian crayfish, Adelaide whiting,
Northern Territory barramundi, Queensland Reef
fish, both sand and mud crabs and Moreton Bay
bugs; but lobsters, prawns, scallops, squid and the
myriad varieties of fish are uniformly good.

Sweets   A Sydney cousin insists that I should cater for the
sweet-toothed with recipes for pavlova, the only

uniquely Australian pudding to have passed into European cuisines, which is a meringue and fruit concoction of great delicacy; lamingtons, a childhood favourite, which are blocks of sponge cake coated with chocolate and shredded coconut; and a very Australian passionfruit icing for a sponge cake. These recipes are at the end of this chapter.

Many of the most interesting parts of Australia to visit are so hot that drinking for pleasure is not always alcoholic. Two of my most memorable drinks were of water – once from a traveller's palm tree, and once in a tropical rainforest alive with calling birds, drinking, then swimming in a pool below a tumbling waterfall. Despite the attractions of Australian lager, the ice-cold 'amber nectar', and the superb wines, I would advise you to drink water and fruit juices in liberal quantities when exposed to the fierce sun for hours. On a long car or coach journey take a melon or oranges with you as well as a carton of juice, and wait until after sundown to savour the wine. Then choose a table overlooking the sea, and one of the two great grapes of Burgundy – Chardonnay or Pinot Noir, evolving to perfection in Australia – and savour the quality.

Wine and other drinks

Soft drinks

Due to climate, soil varieties, technical expertise and freedom from Old World restrictions, Australian wines have the rich flavour of fully ripened grapes with interesting oaking, which is rapidly propelling them upwards into a class of their own. From the Hunter Valley in New South Wales, Tyrrells 1976 Pinot Noir stunned the wine world by being voted world's best Pinot in the illustrious Gault et Milleau wine awards of 1979. The 1981 Pinot Noir is currently the Australian champion, while their 1977 Vat 47 Pinot Chardonnay is still the most successful Chardonnay in Australian wine history. As Tyrrells cater to the top 15 per cent of the market, anything with their label should be a good wine.

Australian Chardonnays generally are currently in such demand overseas that crops of the grape are now commanding huge prices – second only to crops of marijuana, I was told only half-jokingly. There is

Pinot Noir and Chardonnay

a preference for the richer, oakier and fuller-bodied style of Chardonnay, reflected in a recent international wine challenge in London; out of 2500 wines from twenty countries, with only three trophies awarded, one went to the 1986 Simon Whitlam Chardonnay, again from the Hunter Valley. The good news is that not all great Chardonnays are expensive; Seppelts, from the Barossa Valley in South Australia, retails its 1988 Gold Label Chardonnay for only $8 a bottle – a magical wine at that price.

The Barossa Valley typifies the European origins but Australian development of the wine industry: Lutherans fleeing from persecution founded a dynasty there, still German-speaking today, but employing the most modern equipment and expertise. A French wine grower touring the area acknowledged the superior techniques used, observing that if French wine-makers were able to make their wines as scientifically and technically as they do in Australia, instead of by father-to-son methods, there would be a big improvement in French wines. There has been an enormous investment in technical perfection, so that quality is improving constantly. Casking is done at a lower price level than in Europe (excepting Spain), and the combination of cool-climate hillside vineyards, prohibiting mechanical harvesting, with adventurous mixing of varieties of grape promises even better quality in the future.

Other wines   Some Australian labels indicate 'botyritis', the German 'noble rot', and I was surprised to learn that expertise had developed to the extent of producing artificially what occurs naturally in the damp climate of a German hillside to make a splendid Auslese.

The one-grape premium Australian wine, though uniformly rich and full-flavoured, has been criticized in the past for lacking complexity. Now innovative and very interesting blends, not allowed in Europe, are becoming a feature of Australian wines. Rosemount Estate in New South Wales have blended the traditional grape of their area, the Semillon, with Chardonnay very successfully, while the Cape Mentelle Semillon/Sauvignon from Western Australia is remarkable. Both are surprisingly inexpensive.

Even if you can't go on wine-tasting tours of the vineyards, be as adventurous as possible. Some Adelaide hosts consider their Rieslings so good that you need try no other white wine, but a dry white Frontignac is an excellent aperitif and Sauvignon blanc a subtle complement to their famous fish, the sharply sweet whiting. Mellow Cabernet Sauvignons vary from good to outstanding, with deep berry flavours and a long, firm finish. Look out for the 1982 vintage for a special treat.

The Shiraz (Syrah to the rest of the world) grape has come into a kind of grandeur in Australia, either in its own right, full-bodied, opulent and spiced, as in the Mount Avoca Shiraz 1985, or as a beguiling blend with Cabernet Sauvignon. The Brown brothers of Milawa have produced an extraordinary blend of Shiraz, Mondeuse and Cabernet, inky dark, which drinks the way a really ripe Camembert tastes. With further cellaring it could become a classic accompaniment to venison and grouse.

Australia's greatest red wine, originating in the 1950s, is Grange Hermitage. A memorable wine at an affordable price is Tollana Hermitage 1984, with great depth of Shiraz fruit and integrated oak. Wynn's Coonawarra Estate in South Australia is a label to bear in mind. The red soil and cooler climate produce some of the finest Australian wines, including Pinot Noir, Hermitage and Cabernet Hermitage.

Another cool-climate label to look out for is one from near Melbourne, the Yarra Yering. James Halliday, Australia's top wine writer, considers the 1983 Yarra Yering Pinot Noir the best Pinot ever made in Australia. As you would expect, it is the most expensive, but one you will remember from Down Under whenever you hear Australians being disparaged as a nation of beer-swillers.

At the affordable daily end of the market, Penfold's Seaview label is possibly the most popular in Australia, consistently good and extremely reasonably priced.

The Australian wine industry began with fortified wines, and they are well represented under the Kaiser Stuhl label. Port drinkers might look for Berry Estate Fine Old Tawny Port.

Fortified wines and champagne

In the champagne class, it is not every day that one drinks 1982 Dom Perignon or Cordon Rouge, but Minchinbury is one of the oldest and most respected names in the Australian champagne industry, and even the non-vintage champagnes are worthy of a celebration, especially at prices as low as $2 a bottle.

Sitting in the shade of a coolibah tree waiting till the billy boils and the jolly jumbuck cooks is all very well, but for waltzing Matilda a good bottle of wine is better.

Pavlova   *Serves 6–8*

Base   3 egg whites
175 g (6 oz) castor sugar
2.5 ml ($\frac{1}{2}$ teaspoon) cornflour
2.5 ml ($\frac{1}{2}$ teaspoon) vinegar
2.5 ml ($\frac{1}{2}$ teaspoon) vanilla essence

Filling   275 ml (10 fl oz) double or whipping cream
10 ml (2 teaspoons) icing sugar
2.5 ml ($\frac{1}{2}$ teaspoon) vanilla essence
Soft fruit, for example, 225 g (8 oz) strawberries, 4 kiwi fruit and 6 passionfruit

Method   1   Whisk egg whites until very stiff. Beat in sugar gradually, adding cornflour with last addition. Fold in vinegar and vanilla essence.

2   Sprinkle cornflour on greased greaseproof paper on baking tray. Spread meringue mixture into an 18-cm round. Pile meringue to make a pie shell, cake or dome.

3   Bake at 100–120 °C (200–250 °F, gas mark $\frac{1}{4}$–$\frac{1}{2}$) for $1\frac{1}{2}$–2 hours, until crisp and dry.

Pavlova contd.

Cool in oven with oven door open before removing paper.

4   To serve: whip cream until stiff. Add vanilla essence and icing sugar to taste. Pile on top of meringue case, and arrange prepared, sliced fruit over cream.

To vary the filling: use ice cream instead of cream. Use other fresh or tinned fruit, or lemon curd.

Makes 35   **Lamingtons**

Make a buttercake using your own favourite recipe.

45–60 ml (3–4 tablespoons) boiling water   *Icing*
25 g (1 oz) butter
30 ml (2 tablespoons) cocoa
275 g (10 oz) icing sugar
225 g (8 oz) dessicated coconut

1   Keep the cake for at least two days before   *Method*
use.
2   In a bowl over hot water, add boiling water to butter. Mix in cocoa. Beat in sifted icing sugar.
3   Cut cake into 4-cm (1½-inch) squares. Dip each piece in icing, using a long fork, and roll them in coconut. Leave to set on wire rack.

Passionfruit   *Serves 8–10*
sponge

Sponge   4 eggs
Scant 175 g (6 oz) castor sugar
75 g (3 oz) cornflour
25 g (1 oz) plain flour
5 ml (teaspoon) baking powder

Filling   275 ml (10 fl oz) double or whipping cream

Icing   5 ml (teaspoon) melted butter
150 g (5 oz) icing sugar
2 passionfruit

Method   1 To make sponge: separate eggs. Whisk whites until stiff. Beat in sugar gradually. Beat in yolks one at a time. Sift both flours and baking powder together three times and fold into mixture.
2 Divide mixture evenly between two greased and floured 20-cm (8-inch) sandwich tins. Bake at 180–190 °C (350–375 °F, gas mark 4–5) for 20–5 minutes. Cool in tins for 2–3 minutes, then loosen with a knife and cool on wire rack.
3 To fill: whip cream until stiff. Use to sandwich sponges together.
4 To ice: add melted butter to sifted icing sugar. Add juice and pips of passionfruit until icing will spread. Spread over top of sponge.

Getting into entertainment

Australian mates endearingly call each other 'sport', **Sport**
identifying the games they play with the people who
play them. To be ignorant of sport is to be ignorant
of Australia. It is an integral part of the nation's
culture; indeed, not so many years ago, one might
have said its only culture. In a country that has
traditionally shunned bookishness, sport in the great
outdoors is a major social activity, be it playing
tennis, cricket, football or golf, swimming, walking,
cycling, horseriding or sailing. Unlike America,
Australia has few fat people.

For many young people, surfing is a way of life *Surfing*
rather than a sport. It can be a hazard for tourists,
unaware that whole stretches of the sea are reserved
for flying surfers with their lethal boards. All round
Australia, sun and surf reflect the national image of
a cool, healthy, active lifestyle. Visitors can enjoy
seabathing (without the large surf breakers) whenever
they are on the coastline. The danger from sharks is
minimal.

If gambling can be called a sport, the Aussies manage *Gambling*
this national pastime both indoors and out, and combine it, wherever possible, with other sports as spec-
tators. Race meetings are held all over Australia, from
the prestigious Melbourne Cup to the Birdsville Races
in the outback. The tote, or mechanical total-
izer, is an Australian invention, necessary because
the bookies could not cope with the flood of bets
fast enough. In the outback, they also have camel
races, snail races and toad races; even boat races in
Alice Springs without water – the boats are bottom-
less, and people run inside the hulls holding them
up, would you believe. (The 'Northern Territory'
chapter tells you more.)

There are casinos in big cities and illicit gambling dens in the states which, in theory, do not allow gambling. 'Playing the pokies' brings coachloads of people to poker machines. Wherever there are Aussie men, on remote stations in the outback, in shearing quarters or droving camps, they will gamble. Perhaps this is the mysterious 'mateship' link. I have seen a circle of shearers, with a kangaroo dog, following the flight of two pennies for hours at a time, enthralled in two-up betting on whether the sheep were wet or dry for shearing.

Football   In this 'man's country', a 'man's sport' is Aussie rules. Arguably rougher than rugby or American football, Aussie rules is watched by enthralled crowds crying for blood in interstate battles, almost a substitute for war between Queensland and New South Wales.

Rugby, both union and league – particularly the latter – is very popular, although more so amongst people of British descent. Football (that is, soccer) by contrast is played mainly by new Australians. Older families have watched *Match of the Day* from England for many years, but the proliferation of Australian teams is mainly organized by migrants from Europe.

Watersports   Water-related sports are readily available. At every resort where there are facilities for scuba-diving, snorkelling, parasailing, skin-diving, water-skiing, windsurfing and big-game marlin fishing, you will find tuition available. Even if you take off in a parachute only once in your lifetime, it's easier from a standing position on a platform in the sea than it must be from a reckless plane drop, and the joy of floating into the blueness of the sky, with the deeper blue water shimmering below, is near heaven.

The Gold Coast and Barrier Reef resorts are the best places for all forms of watersports, but tend to be expensive. Some hotels in Cairns and Townsville give free snorkelling tuition in their swimming pools before you go out to the Reef on a day's excursion. It is most important that you don't attempt a new watersport without tuition, as some of them can be dangerous.

It may surprise you to realize you can ski in the snowy mountains of New South Wales, but try instead the more uniquely Australian sports of horse-riding in the outback, and all the watersports. Tennis can be played on public courts in almost every part of Australia, and swimming pools are available at motels and hotels. Golf is more difficult for the visitor, as many courses are for members only, but for the dedicated golfer some clubs give temporary membership. Ask the local tourist office for advice on sporting facilities available, and compare prices.

Australians have done well internationally in cricket and tennis, sailing and surfing, athletics generally, golf and bowls, squash and Formula One racing, snooker and swimming, boxing and rowing. As a visitor you will not be able to cover the whole sporting spectrum, but sample some. You will find Aussies very competitive, but also helpful.

Until the sixties, Australia was a cultural desert, and artists of all kinds left the country in droves. What has been termed the 'cultural cringe' about Aussie artistic endeavour ended primarily because of government funding and promotion of the arts. Although Dame Edna Everage is highly sceptical of the 'Yartz' in Australia, there is a lot happening, some of it exploratory, some excellent by international standards.

Abroad, Australian films are a great success, especially documentaries and those giving a slice-of-life perspective. Even Aussie commercials for the 'amber nectar' have caused great merriment – as a diplomat for his country, Paul Hogan has done more to popularize Australia than any politician from Canberra. Australian writers are producing excellent plays and film scripts about their own country instead of importing Noel Coward, and Australian actors are speaking with their own Aussie accents.

Music and dance

To the outside world, the symbol of Australia's creative development is the Sydney Opera House, perhaps the most beautiful modern building in the world. Do not worry if 'Australia' and 'opera' do not trip off the tongue comfortably together; it takes time to get used to, but the Opera House stages all forms of performing arts, including the superb Sydney Dance Company.

Although Sydney and Melbourne are the acknowledged centres for professional work in ballet, music and theatre, in both Brisbane and Adelaide there is growing public support for their performing arts centres. Adelaide hosts a very good festival, and Brisbane is now hungry for all things cultural. The international Exposition, known in Australia as Expo, was recently held in Brisbane as part of the bicentennial celebrations, and so Queenslanders benefited enormously from the varied international cultural imports.

I would agree with them that Morris dancing might well have stayed at home, but the Royal Ballet, the Old Vic, Japanese No theatre, Balinese dancing and brilliant operas and orchestras gave a great impetus to the arts generally in Australia. Australians have always enjoyed good music, but the Yartz generally are no longer spoken of with derision.

Art galleries and museums

Art galleries and museums, even some of the smaller ones, I found interesting and exciting. Darwin was the last place I expected to see anything other than a rock band, but instead there were some of the finest Australian paintings in the country, as well as the best collection of Aboriginal bark paintings. Even in a small coastal town in north Queensland a local man had put together a fascinating exhibition of shipwrecks, with extraordinary items recovered from the early times when great sailing ships had sundered on the Reef.

Television

The crossroads at which Australian culture finds itself is exemplified by television – always an indicator of what the masses really enjoy in entertainment. There are popular American imports – *The Cosby Show*,

Alf, American football, *California Revisited* – and English imports such as *Yes, Minister*, *Rumpole of the Bailey* and *Brideshead Revisited*. Australia also makes its own programmes, such as *Neighbours* and *The Flying Doctors*, as well as good documentaries.

Unfairly, because it is visually a more exciting city and expert at promoting itself, Sydney has an overseas reputation for being the place with a monopoly on Australian culture. Typically underplaying its virtues, Melbourne has wonderful art galleries, museums and old theatres, and its performing arts centre, though outwardly disappointing, is a miracle of modern technology, to be envied anywhere in the world. Its ballet company, concerts and plays offer the best of Australia's vibrant artistic talents.

Cultural centres

In Brisbane also, essentially a country town recently elevated to international status, the narrow-mindedness which stifled artistic expression has been swept away. I saw several new Australian plays there, well staged and performed, drawing on subjects such as the conservation of Dunk Island, a small Barrier Reef island of complex beauty and wildlife, now being rescued from insensitive development.

Adelaide's performing arts centre stages an international festival, attracting very good productions from abroad as well as Australian works. Although a more modest centre than Sydney, it is as solid as Adelaide itself, very functional, and set in beautiful surroundings by the river. Adelaide typifies for me what might be termed the cultural crossroads in Australia; for as well as the great strides – that's progress, not trousers – it has made in the pursuit of culture, it has also glorified its casino. The ex-railway station is a beautiful building of colonial grandeur, its marbled halls far busier than the performing arts centre. Another rival is the annual *bête noire* of local residents, the Adelaide Grand Prix, which attracts thousands of tourists – the noise apparently travels as far as the mountains 40 km away.

Australia, with its new diversity, will probably manage to combine entertainment for all tastes. The

cultural cringe is definitely over. Writers such as
Thomas Keneally, David Williamson, Patrick White
and Peter Carey speak with a uniquely Australian
voice, powerful and true, as did the poets Kenneth
Slessor and Judith Wright. A contagious confidence
is now permeating what was formerly the Yartz. I
believe the best is yet to be.

Getting up a gum-tree: wildlife

When the scientist Charles Darwin first saw the extra-ordinary wildlife of Australia, he speculated on the possibility of there being two Gods: one who had created the rest of the world, and one who had created Australia. Cut off from other landmasses for millions of years, and inhabited solely by the Aborigines, the world's greatest conservationists, the flora and fauna of Australia have developed in their own unique way.

Fossilized footprints of dinosaurs have been found on the coast of Western Australia and in the hills of Victoria; fragments of the skeletons of vast sea leviathans have lain in sandy deserts which were once an inland sea. Today there is a creature left over from the earliest days of evolution, the platypus, often called a living fossil. A mammal which suckles its young, the duck-billed platypus lays eggs, is furry, and yet has webbed feet that enable it to swim easily. This astonishing survivor can be seen, very rarely now, in remote streams in Victoria and New South Wales, and occasionally in captivity in zoos around the world as well as in Australia.

Animal-life

Equally unique as a survivor from the time when creatures evolved into inhabitants of land or water is the lung fish, found in Queensland, which can live and breathe on dry land. Sightings of the platypus and the lung fish are rare but the echidna, or spiny anteater, will obligingly appear, as one did for us in a huge natural garden or 'back yard' in Victoria, digging for insects. Like the platypus, the echidna lays eggs instead of giving birth, and suckles its young. Though it looks like a porcupine, they are not related at all. It and the platypus are considered to be the only two creatures in the world linking reptile and mammal.

Marsupials Of the documented 230 species of mammal in Australia nearly half are marsupials, which have retained a convenient pouch, like a shopping bag, in which their young are carried – easily the most convenient device in the world for mothers. There are marsupials which burrow like the wombat, and those which can't like the numbat, which can only open weak ant and termite nests. There are carnivorous marsupials, such as the Tasmanian Devil and Tasmanian tiger, the latter thought to be extinct. (Early settlers made a clean sweep of Tasmanian Aborigines and tigers.)

As a child, I used to leave a banana every evening for a friendly possum, which used to curl his tail round a branch and swing head first to seize the fruit from a veranda rail.

Kangaroos Because of the scant rainfall in large areas of Australia, the 'survival of the fittest' led to many an evolutionary wonder. The best-known marsupial, the kangaroo, has a built-in system of birth control. In times of drought the female delays growth of the minute embryo implanted on the wall of her uterus, and waits until rains fall before she activates its growth cycle – for more than a year if necessary. In good times, she can be in a continual state of reproduction, with one joey hopping beside her, occasionally suckling, a young joey installed in the pouch drawing her milk, and an embryo in waiting.

Kangaroos have extremely powerful hindquarters, allowing them to travel long distances at speeds of up to 48 km an hour, but there is great carnage on outback roads because they become mesmerized by car-lights. Huge metal grids protect coaches and four-wheel drives, and there are sickening crunches accompanying night driving. Despite the sides of roads in the outback being littered with carcasses, kangaroo shooters are employed for culling.

There are more than 150 species of kangaroo, the red kangaroo being the tallest, above human height, while the wallabies, much smaller, are the ones you see most commonly in captivity. Rat kangaroos and the tiny quokkas of Rottnest Island are the smallest. In captivity wallabies will eat grass from your hand

and sniff inside tourists' bags, while the free-ranging quokkas are singularly importunate, demanding half your picnic.

Koalas Probably the marsupial most loved by visitors is the koala, wrongly called a bear, though it looks like every child's dream of cuddles. The name 'koala' is Aboriginal for 'no water', because the animal obtains its moisture from the oils in the eucalyptus leaves it eats. You can see koalas snoozing high up in the forks of gum trees, because they are nocturnal animals which climb down the trees at night to squabble a bit on the ground before claiming eating rights in the branches of a neighbouring eucalyptus. Should you cuddle one in a koala sanctuary, beware of eucalyptus-smelling urine. Even the British prime minister once escaped being sprayed only by a few centimetres.

Research into koala diseases is being accelerated, because the numbers of those in the wild are dwindling rapidly as a scourge of venereal disease sweeps through their population, making them sterile. Koalas in captivity are generally free of disease.

Bush tucker To us, all the marsupials look like gentle pets, but to the Aboriginal people they are bush tucker, like other animals. If you spend any time with the Tiwi tribe on Melville Island, near Darwin (see 'Northern Territory'), you can watch them hauling a bandicoot out of a hollow log, killing it quickly and throwing it onto a wood fire. Wallabies, possums and goannas (iguanas) are despatched

(Reproduced by kind permission of Sean Leahy and Gerard Piper, © Columbia Features Inc 1989.)

in the same way, providing bush tucker as they have done for 40,000 years.

Flying mammals   There are flying mammals, nocturnal, warm-blooded, furry bats which suckle their young and eat fruit, hanging upside down in colonies in suburban front gardens in Cairns. There is also the rare cannibal bat of central Australia, which has the endearing quality of feeding on its own species.

Reptiles   More likely to feed on you, should you dive into the wrong rivers, are crocodiles. The estuarine crocodile has been protected since 1972, but the increasing number of tourists swallowed in Northern Australia has led to many people demanding more crocodile skins for handbags, and less left to eye visitors voraciously. The Johnston crocodile, a freshwater species, is said to be harmless, but they looked very similar to me. Tourists have swum in Northern Territory rivers believing that only the Johnston family was with them, but estuarine cousins swimming upstream ended their holiday dramatically.

Some of the lizards look menacing, such as the Perentie goanna, the blue-tongued skink and the grotesque frill-necked lizard, but they are all harmless.

There are about a hundred species of snake, but only three are dangerous. Many years ago I knew a boy who thrust one hand into a grape vine while hoeing beneath it. Feeling a stinging sensation he withdrew his hand quickly, to be confronted by a tiger snake still attached to two fingers. I had to grow up with this symbol of outback bravery, because the boy chopped off his fingers with a blunt hoe before walking home to report the incident. Luckily I have never met a tiger snake, a brown snake or the taripan, which is 2 m long. In areas where you might encounter one of these extremely venomous creatures, anti-venom serum is readily available.

Spiders   While I am regaling you with horrors, there are the funnel-web spider and the very tiny red-backed spider to avoid at all costs, but you are unlikely to encounter either of these venomous species, unless

(Reproduced by kind permission of Swamp Productions Pty Ltd.)

you move old logs from a stack in tinder-dry country.

Birds

Bird life in Australia is exotic. You will hear the bushman's alarm clock, the kookaburra; its manic laugh might be disturbing, but it is a great snake-killer. The cockatoos, parrots and parrakeets, budgerigars and kingfishers have such brilliant plumage that the visitor can scarcely believe the splashes of scarlet and green, yellow and white, pink and grey, as they flock a few hundred metres away.

The emu and the cassowary are huge birds, about 1.5 m tall, too heavy to fly, but with running speeds of about 40 km an hour. Emu eggs look like small rugger balls, but dark green and pitted, and are hatched by the male, as are the scrub turkey's offspring.

In the Northern Territory there are so many species of exotic birds that the wetlands might be in a different country from the rest of Australia – 260 species watched over by the sea eagle and the dancing brolgas.

Plant-life

Wetlands and desert

Visitors to the wetlands are astonished by the carpet of water lilies covering lagoons so closely that from a distance they resemble an English meadow sprinkled with daisies rather than a waterway. In the driest part of the continent, however, there is a bigger surprise. In summer there is sand and spinifex, whose roots plunge 10 metres down for moisture; in spring, if rain has fallen, brilliant wild flowers beckon as far as the eye can see, transforming the red desert centre to a wild Australian version of the Dutch tulip fields.

Sturt's desert pea, scarlet and black, and his desert rose, the emblem of the Northern Territory, are magnificent, while the mulga tree puts out huge yellow flowers like bottle brushes. There are everlasting flowers and succulents, fuchsias and a weeping emu bush, colony wattle and grevillea, which all spring amazingly out of the sand.

Witchetty and ti-tree

In limestone country there is the small, yellow-flowering witchetty, a bush, in the roots of which lives the witchetty grub, a delicacy in bush tucker for Aboriginal people.

Found mostly along water courses is the ti-tree, whose flowers produce a natural oil with marvellous curative properties, used by Aborigines for centuries. If bushmen were feeling 'a bit crook' they sprinkled a few leaves of the ti-tree into their billy when making tea, instead of the more usual tangy eucalyptus leaves.

Eucalyptus and wattle

The eucalyptus, or gum tree, is an evolutionary wonder just as much as the platypus is. Not only is the eucalyptus resistant to fire, but it actually rises, phoenix like, from the flames – new leaves sprout from charred trunks, with the undergrowth conveniently cleared for the gum tree to receive more light and water. There are hundreds of different varieties, all infinitely adaptable, some of which have been exported to arid zones in South Africa, the US, Japan and the Middle East. Blue gums and the ghostly whites stand like sentinels on the plains, reaching great heights, but there are smaller, flowering varieties. One of these, the erythrocrys, has a vicious characteristic. In Adelaide we got off a tram to photograph one of these trees, which was studded with brilliant red flowers opening from green pods. Suddenly I was in agony; fierce thorns from the pods lying beneath the tree had pierced through rubber soles and penetrated my feet. As a tourist repellent it is surefire. I don't know what it does to birds.

The wattle, with its daffy little yellow balls of colour, is on Australia's national coat of arms, and is prolific everywhere in the country, in hundreds of varieties. Not allowed chewing gum as children, we used to take the natural gum from an incision in the bark of a wattle tree, and chew happily.

From those days I remember the splendour of the rainforests, with bell-birds calling and whip-birds lashing, the shy bushbaby with enormous brown eyes peeping out, and the exquisite lyre bird, its tail feathers spread like a harp. I cannot remember being told about Aboriginal sacred places, but imagine I knew, or felt, a great presence in those cathedral-like trees and rushing cataracts, sometimes benign and sometimes terrifying.

Rainforests

Today the rainforests are pillaged and robbed – rare orchids and plaited tassle ferns are almost extinct. No trees stand where once they cut off the sky. The federal government is attempting to make the surviving rainforests of Queensland world heritage listings, against fierce local opposition. There is a highly organized, though illegal, trade in rare species of plants and birds, for which the rainforests have been a lucrative hunting ground. There are also strong local timber felling, mining and farming interests, not to mention the tourist facilities entrepreneurs, all of whom believe they 'own' the land and have a vested right in developing it as they see fit.

Elsewhere in Australia, as in Europe and America, destruction of the forests has been systematic to clear huge areas for grazing and crop production. The introduction of hoofed animals into Australia destroyed the indigenous ground covering, hastening soil erosion and expanding deserts. Two hundred years since European colonization is a short time in the history of Australia, but for the native flora and fauna, it must have been like a long, long war.

In the wild, kangaroos and wallabies are seen from the road or train as soon as you leave the coast along the eastern seaboard. Koalas are sighted for you in the wild in Tasmania, but are only readily viewed in zoos on the mainland – try the Lone Pine Koala Sanctuary in Brisbane. Taronga Park in Sydney and the Melbourne Zoo have a good, representative collection of marsupials, and zoos in Tasmania have the Tasmanian Devil.

Best places to visit

Marsupials

Birds The Blue Mountains near Sydney, the Dandenong ranges in the south and Mount Tambourine near Brisbane all have colourful, exotic birds, mostly parrots and parrakeets, readily feeding nearby. For birds such as the lyre bird and the bush turkey you need to be on a guided tour of a rainforest. Visit Kakadu National Park too, and both Taronga Park and the Melbourne Zoo have good collections of birds.

Platypuses It is most unusual to see a platypus in a Victorian or New South Wales stream now, but campers are occasionally lucky. My best advice is to go to the zoo and the botanical gardens of the capital city you arrive at, and then ask the local tourist office for guided tour information, as it changes frequently.

Marine and river life For marine life, visit the Barrier Reef from Cairns, or go to the reef that has been re-created indoors in Townsville. For crocodiles in the wild visit Kakadu National Park. They are in captivity in small zoos outside Cairns, where a keeper entertains the crowd by banging with a wire rake beside a pool until the crocodile lunges for him; whereupon a dead hen (still feathered) is thrown into its open jaws. Some tourists love it.

Getting on with Australians

In Australia today the predominant stock is that of an island people descended from an older island people. Insularity is bred in the bone. Japanese people would recognize this trait, and perhaps empathize. Being born on an island, whatever its size, isolates the islander from 'foreigners' – and that means anyone not born on their island.

The prejudices of the old island were brought to the new, reinforced, even, by the strangeness of the southern hemisphere, the vastness of the island continent, and the feeling that they were a long way from mother. The new Australians tried, desperately hard, to remain British.

If those early settlers were to come back to Australia today they would be amazed by the multicultural fizz, the entrepreneurial sparkle, which is nevertheless allied with something of those frontier days – the pioneering spirit. Australians have forged a new national identity, not altogether willingly, but propelled by forces over which they have little control. The outside world is coming to live in their island. The children of 'foreigners' are Australians.

I was speaking to the daughter of an Italian migrant who had achieved high office in Australia, and asked if there were any problems at her school in assimilating new migrant children. Surprised, she said, 'Why should anyone think they are better than anyone else?' Wisdom does indeed come out of the mouths of babes and sucklings. Her viewpoint is indicative of the new-look Australia. Sadly, it is not everywhere in the country. The average Australian of British stock is more openhearted than openminded.

Bear that girl's reply in mind when your first impression of Australians is of the one who enters your plane on the tarmac at Sydney, complete with **First impressions** mask and spray, and fumigates you before you set foot on the soil. It really is necessary to kill any stowaway insects, not because he thinks all foreigners are dirty and don't take enough showers.

Going through immigration control, you will notice that officials are courteous, in an offhand sort of way, and they wear shorts with long socks. Nobody says 'G'day'. It is dawn, yet there are mobs of Australians waiting to meet passengers, looking casual and laid-back, as if on holiday. This is an enviable national characteristic. They really are far less stressed than their European counterparts. They take life more easily.

If you ask a bus driver if you can be dropped near your hotel, the reply will probably be 'No worries', and he means it. Bus drivers will do their bit in looking after you, cheerfully and laconically. If you take a taxi, the odds are that the driver will be an immigrant with an extraordinary accent but nevertheless an Australian, born in Greece or Italy perhaps, who has absorbed the laid-back, egalitarian attitudes of the older Aussies. The driver will expect you to sit in the front, beside him, and talk. Enjoy it for the open, friendly welcome it is. What's more, the fare will be reasonable, and the driver doesn't expect a tip. Nobody in Australia has his or her wages subsidized by the customer in tips, so whether they are taxi-drivers, waitresses or hairdressers, they perform their jobs without the subservient, sometimes obsequious attitude noticeable in those who need tips to live. Australians believe in upholding the dignity of each individual's work, to me one of their best qualities.

Hospitality If approached in the right way, their friendliness and hospitality are as sunny as the climate. It is not unusual for an Australian to offer to entertain you for a day or a weekend, longer if they live in the outback, simply after a couple of hours' conversation while travelling. Don't be nervous of accepting these spontaneous invitations. They are genuinely hospitable people who are delighted to share their free time with you.

Then of course you will praise the beaches, the sunshine, the friendliness of the people, the excellent food and wine; in deeper discussions, tread warily on sensitive topics such as the treatment of the Aborigines, the role of the crown (past as in the removal of Fraser as prime minister, future as in the removal of said crown in favour of a republic), increasing the immigrant quota, and corruption in government and police.

Listen to the Australian point of view, and be careful to discuss, not criticize. It always used to be said that Australians had a chip on their shoulder about national criticism (don't we all?), but on the whole you will find them more open and balanced now they have absorbed so many different nationalities, comparatively painlessly.

Though national criticism is to be avoided, the exception to this is that you are expected to join in the criticism of one state by another, rather like children squabbling in their family. Interstate rivalry in Australia is intense, so diplomatic visitors praise whatever they can, honestly, in the state in which they find themselves, but never praise another state at the expense of the one they're in.

Interstate rivalry

This applies particularly to the rival cities of Melbourne and Sydney. Praising Sydney to a Melbournite puts you beyond the pale, certainly beyond the barbie, and vice versa; but the biggest mistake to make socially in either of those cities is to praise Queenslanders. It's all right to admire Queensland's physical geography, such as the Barrier Reef, its islands and beaches, but stay silent after that, for everything Queensland represents is 'fascist' to the south – similar to New York or Washington regarding the 'redneck' Southern states as being reactionary and racist.

Needless to say, when in Queensland say nothing of all this. Individually, Queenslanders are kind, warm and hospitable; collectively, the old, narrow attitudes die hard. With so much foreign investment, particularly Japanese, coming into Australia, racist attitudes are changing. The best way to get on with

the more conservative people is to allay their sus-
picions first. Queenslanders particularly resent outside interference and criticism, and fear any change
in the status quo. If you are investing there, go
slowly. Get to know the local people, talk to them,
explain how they may benefit from your plans, and
how you wish to fit in with them. Prejudice dies
slowly, and they are afraid that immigrants with alien
customs will destroy their way of life.

If investing in Australia, regard Kimihito Kamori
as your role model. A Japanese conservationist, he
recently bought Lone Pine Koala Sanctuary in Brisbane. There was a great public outcry until he
explained that living conditions for the koalas would
be vastly improved, with research set up to prevent
koala diseases, and tourist facilities modernized. With
great charm, he won over his critics with 'I don't
really own the Lone Pine koalas – the people of
Australia own them.'

**Your own
attitude**

Be enthusiastic about Australia, and Aussies will
respond generously. It is always a reciprocal relation-
ship of one kind or another. We had been enthralled
by a wonderful museum and art gallery in Darwin,
the curator happy to fill in the history of the Macassans (see 'Northern Territory') and Aborigines. At
closing time monsoonal rain fell in sheets, pounding
the tropical trees. There were no taxis, no public
transport. 'Come', said the curator. 'Come with me
to Darwin's Raffles Hotel, and I'll tell you more over
a drink.' We drove through the downpour until it
stopped as suddenly as it had begun. In the hotel's
gracious twenties setting, beneath huge planters' fans,
we relaxed and talked, before the curator drove us
to our hotel.

I could go on endlessly about the kindness of
strangers I met in Australia, but what I want you to
understand is that the magic won't happen if your
attitude to Aussies you meet is reserved and cold.
Whatever your race, try to shed your inhibitions in
Australia. Respond to the openness of the country,
and the people; large spaces breed expansive people.
Your interest and enthusiasm should be demonstrated

vocally. If you are silent there is no feedback for the guides – extremely knowledgeable people who will give as much, or little, information on the tour as their audiences appear to want.

If you are invited to a party or barbecue, you might witness a strange Aussie convention, luckily extinct in more cosmopolitan circles. The host and hostess do not mingle, introducing guests and making sure no-one is left out. Instead, there is a ritual stampede as the sexes are segregated, men to one end of the room, women to the other.

Gender apartheid

Australian women were the first in the world to be enfranchised, and proved themselves to be strong in adversity in the old pioneering days. My grand-mother, for example, used to travel with my grand-father in bullock drays to set up camp in some remote part of the bush, while my grandfather surveyed a railway. There was a photograph of her, a tiny slen-der figure in a dark crinoline, with whalebone collar and a cameo brooch, seated at a piano, of all things, in a bush clearing. By her feet were several small children. My grandfather, in stiff white collar, was conducting divine service for two embarrassed lines of men, standing on opposite sides; white on one, Aboriginal on the other. That frail-looking little woman went on to have ten children, and accompanied my grandfather wherever she could, an equal partner, a true helpmate.

Many Australian women now, however, are singu-larly acquiescent in being treated as appendages or ornaments (the ones you don't see are the workhorses). So what has happened in Australia to create the present unnatural gender apartheid, when the two sexes enjoyed such a wonderful equality of sharing in the pioneering days?

Perhaps it was that overrated 'mateship', so often quoted as the basis for understanding Aussies. I think the mateship concept is nonsense. In the early days of colonization men outnumbered women by four to one, so obviously the mates had to stick together, helping each other to tame the wilderness. Today the mates live mostly in towns, with no shortage of women or anything else, and choose to segregate the sexes because they are socially uneasy with women or afraid of losing some absurd macho image of a 'real man'. If you are a male visitor, join the women. They'll love it.

Joining in

If you have a good sense of humour, you'll get on well with Australians. You will meet many a sharp wit, which initially might be construed as cruel, but if you give as good as you get, great hilarity is enjoyed by all, and you will be respected for it. Australians enjoy a good laugh at their own expense, as well as yours.

Wherever possible, join in the fun of some sporting event, the more way-out the better. If you prefer to be a spectator, lay a bet on your favourite to win. Aussies bet on anything, from snail to camel racing, and from men to lizards drinking. The current beer drinking record at a remote Northern Territory pub is held by a Brahmin bull.

Because the climate is so marvellous, most Australians in cities spend as much time as possible out of doors. It is never a trouble for them to include one or two visitors from abroad in a day at the beach, playing tennis or at one of their famous barbies in the back yard (garden). They appreciate directness. Ask if it's possible to join them in a casual way. Formality does not sit easily on Aussie shoulders.

One of the best ways to establish a friendly, hospitable environment is to offer a reciprocal arrangement. Many Australians travel abroad, especially the young ones, and they and their parents appreciate an address in Europe, Asia or America. If you are friendly and open with Australians, you cannot fail to enjoy them, as well as their country.

Getting bushed: the Aborigines

The most ancient continent on earth, Australia is also the driest. It was not always so. In the days of prehistory there was a great inland sea in the centre of the Australian landmass and a more equable climate. One of the earliest forms of mankind (Mungo man) emerged round the shores of the inland sea, only to disappear with the bathwater when, in a vast upheaval of nature, the inland sea became desert.

Some 40,000 years ago the first migrants came to fill the vacuum: the Aborigines, crossing by land bridges from the north and northwest. With the rise of sea levels the land bridges disappeared and the Aborigines were left alone to evolve into the indigenous people of Australia, comprising many different tribes speaking some 200 languages, developing distinctive physical attributes, but sharing a common religious belief – the land was a sacred trust and everything therein, both animate and inanimate, was to be conserved.

A mystical, nomadic people, their creation myth is as awesome as those of other religions. In the beginning, or from the 'Dreamtime', came their progenitors, sacred totemic beings who created all things. They walked across the continent singing into existence everything that crossed their paths – calling it up from the earth by name – each rock, each creek, each gully, every animal, bird or tree, the animate and the inanimate.

These journeys of the Ancestors form myriads of invisible pathways meandering across the country, minutely detailed, as in an ordnance survey map. The difference is that they are not written or drawn, but sung in couplets, handed down from one generation to the next.

Dreamtime and the Ancestors

Getting bushed: the Aborigines

To follow in the footprints of the Ancestor is to observe the way of the law. An Aborigine has his own family name, such as Muraburra, and his totemic identity, such as a wallaby or emu or honey ant man, the latter determined by which Ancestor's footprints his mother stood in when she first felt the quickening of life within her. The child is born into his spiritual heritage, and is taught gradually the rhyming couplets describing his Ancestor's journey, so that he too can 'sing up' the land, knowing in advance what terrain to expect, ensuring his survival as he crosses the continent in search of plentiful game, a water-hole, or a wife.

He is given his tjuringa, an oval plaque made of stone or mulga wood, on which is carved the journey of his Ancestor. One is reminded of other tablets of stone on which was written the law, for this tjuringa represents the soul of the Aborigine and the immortal soul of the Ancestor, to whom he will return at death – into the Dreamtime.

Over 200 languages were once spoken, but nothing is written down, because of the secret, and indeed sacred, nature of their knowledge, so by a prodigious feat of memory the holy law is kept alive in song.

For the Aborigines to continue in the footsteps of the Ancestor, the land must remain unchanged; for the progress of Western civilization, construction and mining must go ahead. This is the modern dilemma. To what extent should land be given back to the Aboriginal people? To what extent can they rebuild their ancient identity and be protected from further injustices?

**The past and
today**

No-one can undo the shameful history of the treatment of Aborigines over the last 200 years, still largely omitted from Australian history taught in schools, but at least that history is now being openly acknowledged.

There was a total genocide of the Aboriginal people who once inhabited Tasmania – perhaps 5000 people – countless more from the eastern seaboard, and whole tribes from every other area in Australia, as white settlement advanced. As early as 1857 a Commons Select Committee called for an end to 'atrocities against the Australian natives'. As late as 1988 a Royal Commission was set up to examine the alarming rate of deaths among Aborigines in custody, and proposed that police investigations of Aborigines found dead in prison cells should presume homicide, not suicide, as was formerly the case. Western Australia, the state with the highest number of custody deaths, has taken legal action to try to close down the enquiry.

Crime rates

Although they form less than 2 per cent of the population, Aborigines comprise up to 15 per cent of prisoners in some states, mainly due to drunkenness and related offences. The commission calls for the abolition of public drunkenness as an offence, and for task forces to be set up to deal with Aboriginal social and health problems created by alcohol. It further advocates tightening screening in police and prison officer recruitment to eliminate racists, and officer training courses, with examinations, on Aboriginal history, culture and social behaviour. So far, these are only proposals, but if made law they would have far-reaching effects in protecting Aboriginal people.

Land rights

A land rights movement has been instrumental in securing the return of certain territories to Aborigines, such as Ayers Rock and parts of Kakadu National Park in the Northern Territory, but as these places are valuable as tourist attractions, the Aboriginal people do not 'own' them outright. Those tribes indigenous to the area receive a part share in the income generated by tourism, and theoretically are able to return to their former way of life in small, designated areas. Tourists pay for guided Aboriginal tours in Queensland rainforests, islands off the northwest and parts of the Northern Territory.

Land rights for Aborigines is often a misnomer. Even when land is returned to them, as was the case with the Rudall River National Park in the interior of Western Australia, they are powerless to stop mining exploration on their land. CRA, an affiliate of the British mining company Rio Tinto Zinc (RTZ), recently announced the discovery of a huge lode of uranium there. The company wants to dispossess the Aboriginal people and mine the uranium.

As controversy grows, the Rudall River Project has been called 'a three act nightmare . . . uranium in a National Park, and on Aboriginal land'. One would like to think that the old style of British colonization of Australia has ceased, and that a British company would not be allowed to mine Aboriginal land, but RTZ has a powerful lobby.

Resettlement   The main difficulty in 'resettling' Aboriginal people is that they must remain in one place, which is of course against their nomadic way of life. They have now been given the vote, and large welfare payments. The latter has led to terrible health problems: many Aborigines are housed in insanitary conditions, unemployed, but with welfare money to be spent on alcohol and Western-style food. There is a high infant mortality rate, even from measles, and life expectancy in an Aboriginal male has been lowered to 32 years.

In towns their situation is aggravated by almost total unemployment, but there is a strong movement generated by educated Aboriginal people to set up their own schools and health centres, and manage their own affairs, which would revolutionize their present inability to be accepted and assimilated into urban communities. Some Aboriginal children, generally from a happy and stable environment, have proved to be intelligent and gifted linguists, but the majority of those from very deprived backgrounds (as with all children) do not respond well in competitive, academic schools. In poor country areas they are perceived to have too much welfare money, while still being disparaged because of the antisocial behaviour of some of their kin.

The second-class citizen label sticks. Many Australians will tell you that all Aboriginal people get drunk, chop up their furniture for firewood, and destroy not only a house, but a 'decent' neighbourhood, by allowing any number of Aboriginal people to move in with them, throwing beer cans in the garden. It is incomprehensible to the average Australian that Aborigines believe that nothing is 'owned'; everything is shared. Assimilation takes time. The urban Aborigine is a displaced person, and his 'place' no longer exists.

Effects on nomadic life

For the traditional, nomadic Aborigines, the biggest current threat is from mining. In the Rudall River area of Western Australia, RTZ has consistently ignored Aboriginal land rights, with apparent impunity. Those tribes who were previously free to live their nomadic life in desert country unwanted for white settlement now face being forced onto settlements – the end of their nomadic way of life also. To add to Aboriginal difficulties, the Western Australian police are notorious for their harassment of Aboriginal people and are presently the subject of an enquiry into the deaths in custody of young Aboriginal men.

In the 1950s and 1960s Britain tested nuclear devices near Maralinga, in South Australia. Ex-servicemen affected by the tests have received compensation; but the claims of Aborigines have been ignored.

Public opinion

Australian public opinion about the plight of the Aborigines is changing slowly. When Captain Phillip landed in Australia in 1788, it was declared an 'uninhabited land.' It is hoped that the Australian government can be persuaded to make a treaty with the original inhabitants, which would formalize their land claim rights.

In fairness to the Australian government, it should be said that, as a matter of statistics, there are now 23,000 Aboriginal students at the secondary level receiving government assistance, a programme begun in 1967, and many thousands of urban families have been housed. Basically, Australians believe in 'fair goes for all'. Now the nature of Aboriginal spiritual beliefs is beginning to be understood by other Australians, it is not impossible that they too should become conservationists, and tune into 'the song that still remains which names the land over which it sings'.

The next eight chapters could have the general title 'Getting familiar: the states and Australian Capital Territory'. Each chapter goes into some detail on one state or territory, dealt with in the geographical order most logical for visitors starting in the northeast.

Queensland

On a cold London morning while queuing to have my baggage checked for bombs, I began talking, as is my Aussie wont, to a couple also awaiting the airport frisk. They were agog with wonderment at having won a dream holiday to Australia, and bombarded me with questions about the Great Barrier Reef and the outback, Aboriginal rock paintings and bush stockmen. Apart from proving that those fabulous competitions are not rigged, it confirmed my feeling that the 'real Australia' of visitors' dreams could be found almost entirely in Queensland.

Four times the size of Great Britain or Japan, and twice that of Texas, the state of Queensland is almost one quarter of Australia. It encompasses coastline, 5200 km of fine white sand, with the Great Barrier Reef and its myriad islands extending all the way north from the Tropic of Capricorn; rainforests of awesome beauty with tumbling waterfalls; deserts and saltpans; mountains older than life; sunburnt plains with sheep and cattle stations; and a cool temperate area.

History

Queensland has always been sparsely populated. For some 40,000 years, Aboriginal people of many different groupings lived there, and lived well – food was in abundance. Captain Cook remarked on the fine physique and remarkable speed of a tribe on the northeast coast; but fierce battles, such as those fought with the Kalkadoons over mining in their sacred sites in the Mount Isa area, and a gradual dying out through dispersement from their lands, has eliminated untold numbers.

Today you can visit Aboriginal people living in a rainforest in the Daintree area, and learn something of their skills in healing with herbs and roots, as well as being shown bush tucker, including delicious wild fruits and honey. I refused an invitation to uncoil a snake from a mangrove root with my foot – very good bush tucker – but had I been born an Aboriginal woman, doubtless I would simply have brought home the supper.

Sheep and cattle

With the coming of British settlers – the first penal colony was founded near the present site of the capital, Brisbane, in 1824 – the provision of European tucker became a prime necessity. Land was brought under cultivation and hoofed animals introduced, changing the ecology of Queensland, as indeed it has changed that of the entire country. Waving plains of wheat, vast holdings of one sheep to an acre, cattle stations as large as English counties and huge sugar-cane plantations built Queensland into a rich, primary producing state. For many years the sheep's back was the most important source of wealth, but mining also brought men eager to hack their way through rainforests or toil in arid areas to disinter precious metals. Ports were established, roads and railways built, and the first hardy pioneers, in little more than three generations, had tamed and changed the land.

Town and bush

In that vast area, even after the advent of rail communication, small communities were still so isolated that a great distinction became apparent between those Australians who lived in towns and the hardy breed of bush people who hauled supplies to their remote stations twice a year, making new tracks after each flooding. Conditions were harsh, but they bred a race of people self-reliant even today, noticeably different from the urban Aussie. There is a Stockman's Hall of Fame in Longreach, built by national sponsorship, to honour these people.

Curiously enough, Longreach was also the first base for the famous flying doctor service, now used so extensively in Australia. Being able to rely on speedy medical help made a great difference to people in the outback, as did the school of the air, a two-way radio link with the teacher which enables isolated children to receive an education comparable to that provided for town children.

Political attitudes

Always an ultra-conservative state politically, Queensland is notorious in Australia for its repressive and racist attitudes, rooted in its original Protestant/Catholic intolerance transported from Ireland. In Brisbane there used to be a sign outside one factory declaring 'No Protestants need apply', and in the heyday of European immigration individual firms sponsored migrants, unofficially of course, according to religious bias. Italian migrants were admitted in large numbers to work in the cane fields in the tropical north, but there has been marked antipathy to non-British immigration generally, particularly to that of Asians. In fairness to Queenslanders, it should be said that they lost many men in Japanese prisoner-of-war camps in World War II, and but for American intervention would have been invaded by the Japanese.

It is difficult for conservative Queenslanders to accept change of any kind. It would never come from within. A state government considered by many Australians to be extremely hard right, and a police force riddled with corruption, have only recently been challenged. Queenslanders' narrow-mindedness is proverbial; genteel wealth seeks to preserve the status quo by ignoring social issues. An Australian judge, after visiting Toomelan, an Aboriginal community outside Brisbane, described its overcrowded and insanitary conditions, including sewage in open ponds, as being like a Nazi concentration camp. Brisbane is currently involved in the Great Controversy of whether sex education (hiss) should be allowed to enter its schools.

Tourism

Despite their in-built resistance to change, however, Queenslanders are finding their parochialism increasingly difficult to preserve, due to the enormous influx of foreign visitors, with different outlooks, demands and expectations. Wealth generated from the fleeces of sheep was given a conservative brand; wealth generated from the fleeces of tourists must carry the stamp of international thinking.

The tourist industry will have far-reaching effects upon Queensland. It began slowly. Australians from prosperous Sydney and Melbourne discovered that

the 'banana benders' enjoyed a dream-life of golden
beaches, exotic fruits and sunshine whose light was
turned off only for the night stars. Southerners
retired in droves to Queensland. Very soon it became
the Sunshine State with a swinging Gold Coast and
a Sunshine Coast, a Sugar Coast and a Hibiscus
Coast, a Rum City, Australia's Hawaii and its Outback by the Sea. Hotels, houses and holiday resorts,
with games from gambling to parasailing, whole
islands of high-rise termite building, arose with a
rapidity to rival another Creation. As the brochures
say, the climate is beautiful one day, perfect the next.

Travel   A combination of Australia's year-long celebration
of its bicentenary, Expo in Brisbane (see 'Getting in
to entertainment'), and the success of Paul Hogan's
Crocodile Dundee films and 'throw another shrimp
on the barbie' advertisements has created a huge international market for tourism. Like any other industry
in its infancy, there are teething troubles. Most Americans want to see the Barrier Reef, the bush and
Sydney, starting or finishing their tours in Cairns.
Unfortunately, Qantas has only two flights a week
between Cairns and the US. There are two other
international airports at Brisbane and Townsville, and
direct internal flights to practically all the notable
towns and resorts in Queensland.

Unless you book a comprehensive package tour,
however, where all your flights and accommodation
are booked for you, there can be enormous difficulties in finding both seats and beds. Whether you are
travelling to Queensland by plane, rail, coach or car,
book well in advance. If possible, avoid the school
holiday periods of Easter plus the following week,
the middle of June, the last week in September, the
first week in October and from mid-December to
the end of January.

Planning   Airlines, railways and coaches all offer wide-ranging
variants within their price structures, so spend time
planning your mode of travel. Unlike Tasmania,
where a car is essential, Queensland is better enjoyed

by plane hops augmented by rail or coach, using a centre such as Cairns or Townsville, from which you can make excursions to the Reef, the rainforests and the outback. Don't attempt to see all these wonders in a few days; unless you have at least a month to spend in Queensland, decide on either north Queensland or south Queensland with Brisbane and the Gold or Sunshine Coast.

Commercialism has run riot on the Gold Coast, where the main industry is tourism, and offers a Disney-style theme park, a wave pool, the world's longest double-loop rollercoaster, a twenty-four-hour casino and skyscraper blocks intimidating the ocean. Accommodation ranges from five-star hotels of international standard down to camping grounds. You can take an internal flight to Coolangatta, or travel by road from Brisbane. The nightlife out-glitters the sundrenched beaches, but you can escape inland to a national park, with waterfalls and rainforest.

North Queensland is currently suffering from an imbalance caused by very expensive tourist developments, such as Hamilton Island, which is the only place I encountered in Australia where tipping was expected – despite the island's rapacious prices. Its other dubious distinction was its awful coach tour guide and its zoo, both uncharacteristic of Australia. Diseased, half-starved kangaroos and wallabies did not share in the riches of that resort.

Accommodation

There are islands, such as Palm Bay, with reasonably priced accommodation, while camping permits are issued by the rangers' office for uninhabited islands, most of which are national parks. There are excellent value-for-money motels on the mainland, mostly with pools, but book as far in advance as possible.

I was impressed by the locations and amenities of the youth hostels and Backpackers inns. For only $6 per night young people share rooms or dormitories and get discounts on trips to the Reef.

Tours and excursions

Whichever centre you choose, take advantage of the excellent day coach tours, with informative driver/

guides. Each day can be eventful. All coach companies collect passengers from their hotels and motels and take them to the wharf for excursions to the Reef, and return them in the evening – likewise for day trips along the coast or into the hinterland. Leave the booking of your day tours until you arrive at your centre, and take advice on the best operators from your hotel/motel managers, who will generally book them for you.

Remember to protect yourself from the sun, stinging insects and sharp coral, and be advised before you dive carelessly into rivers – many have crocodiles – or even the ocean, since there is a season when you can be stung by the venomous box jellyfish. Take instruction before snorkelling, scuba diving, parasailing or any of the water-related sports, and you'll have a marvellous time. All the reputable Reef day cruises carry an expert, who might even be persuaded to lend you his oyster knife. I was lucky enough to slurp about two dozen oysters from the rocks on an uninhabited island, as well as feeling like superwoman as I snorkelled for long distances. (You'd be surprised how flippers make even inexpert swimmers look like champions.)

The ultimate in luxury is to do an air safari with Aircruising Australia, which flies parties of forty through the red gorges and ranges of the outback and the green jungle wilderness of Cape York, idly dropping into cattle stations and resorts. Do not despair if this is outside your budget, as coaches or four-wheel drive vehicles take you to similar areas, with the advantage of seeing the country more intimately.

Station holidays   For a taste of outback life there are twenty-four station holidays (don't be alarmed: 'station' has no connection with trains, but is Aussie for 'ranch' or 'farm'). Some offer very tame entertainment, like tennis and bushbabies, so read the description of facilities carefully.

If you were enthralled by *Crocodile Dundee* try Dorunda cattle station in the Gulf Savannah, in far-north Queensland. You'll find plenty of wildlife, including crocodiles, as you go on safari with optional extras such as pig-shooting, bird-watching, fishing, watching a cattle-muster, seeing horses being broken in, boating, swimming and camping out. Guests can travel to Normanton by coach, or fly to an all-weather airstrip. It's an opportunity to wear a hat, either swathed in scarves or dangling with corks, but don't be surprised when you're laughed at.

Outback humour is the best in Australia. There is a story of a Texan boasting about the size of his ranch to a Queenslander who owned a station the size of Wales. 'If I rode all day and the following night I still wouldn't have reached my own boundary', drawled the Texan. 'Yeah', said the squatter, 'I know the problem. I had a horse like that once.'

Humour and public institutions

The Australian Law Institute Journal recounts a case of a Queensland farmer suing for damages after he and his horse had been hit by a car. The defence

'There's old age for you! Already this year I've forgotten half of their names!'

(Reproduced by kind permission of Douglas E. Tainsh)

counsel made the striking point that after the accident the farmer had claimed he'd never felt better in his life, so the plaintiff's counsel asked the farmer to explain the circumstances. 'Well', said the farmer, 'soon after the accident my horse was thrashing around with broken legs, and a policeman came up and put his revolver to my horse's ear, and shot him dead. Then he went over to my dog, howling in pain with a broken back, put his revolver to my dog's ear, and shot him dead. Then he came over to me and asked, 'How do you feel?'

The police Police jokes are rife, with corruption evident in the police force from high to low, involving rake-offs from illicit gambling and dubious 'escort' agencies. One visitor complained about his treatment, and demanded to call the police, only to discover that the establishment ripping him off had been set up by two local policemen. Young visitors driving old bangers into Queensland should be careful not to fall foul of the police, because they tend to suspect people without material trappings.

The church The church, too, holds an ambiguous position. In theory private schools, equivalent to British public schools, are all run by the different Christian denominations, but only 3 per cent of Queenslanders are practising Christians. Vietnamese refugees are, for the most part, unwelcome in Queensland, but returned servicemen from the Vietnam war, in conjunction with one of the churches, help them settle. On the whole the established church is trying, somewhat uneasily, to revamp its image. Strains of 'Jesus Christ, Superstar' can be heard from a funeral service, and the beautiful language of ancient services has been thrown out altogether.

In Brisbane I attended a wedding where the spiritual input from the minister was nil – the young couple heard no address, received no blessing on their union. As if we had been audience to a song-and-dance routine instead of witnessing solemn vows, we were asked to put our hands together, not in prayer, but in applause: 'Now let's have a big clap for the bride and groom!' Astonished, I complied, but at the reception queried the devaluation of the priestly role to that of an avuncular master of ceremonies and asked if this was usual in Queensland churches. 'Oh yes', said the minister, taking another glass of champagne. 'We don't have any of that old sermon stuff now. We had two extras, the readings and a song. That's enough. We like our services short and snappy here.'

Queenslanders are not easy to understand. As if in reparation for the shortcomings of the church, speeches at the reception revealed such a warmth and loving kindness, a spiritual affirmation of belief in the couple's future, that I was very moved. The public image in Queensland is a razzmatazz of commercialism, police corruption and civil philistinism, but the private image can be very different.

You will meet a fair cross-section of Australian attitudes in Queensland, both the best and the worst. If you ignore the more rapacious resorts and visit less 'developed' areas you are more likely to meet friendly, gregarious people who will be happy to take you out for a day, or show you how to get water from a traveller's palm tree, service from sleepy hotels or a soothing sunburn lotion. As a banana bender myself, I believe the bunches are growing straighter than they were.

New South Wales

When the new colony was named, it might have been called Llanfairpwllgwyngyllgogerychwyrndrob-wllllantysiliogogogoch, the longest place-name in Wales, but luckily the colonists' nostalgic hankering for Britain, referred to as 'home' by three generations of Australians, was satisfied by a more pronounceable 'New South Wales'. It is indeed, as soap packets proclaim, a new, improved version of South Wales. Before the hills of Sydney, now the capital, were covered by high-rise offices and suburban clusters, they must have looked like the beautiful folds of 'old' South Wales, but today there is no resemblance.

Sydney Sydney is one of the most sparkling cosmopolitan cities in the world, set in a harbour of intricate inlets and vast expanses whose natural grandeur is on the usual Australian scale – mammoth, as in Ayers Rock, the largest monolith in the world, or as in the Great Barrier Reef, the largest living entity in the world. If world heritage listings had been around in the first half of the twentieth century, a great deal of 'development' in Victoria, New South Wales and Queensland would never have happened, but on the whole Sydney is an exception, a multicultural sea city enhanced by Sydney Harbour Bridge and one of the most poetic modern buildings in the world, Sydney Opera House. In a harbour of scudding sails, the Opera House appears wind-lifted between water and sky.

The bicentenary festivities were quite rightly celebrated in Sydney. With only 1 per cent of the population living in the so-called 'real' Australia of the outback, the overwhelming majority of its inhabitants are urban Aussies, working in offices and commuting from the suburbs. As an incredible 20 per cent of all Australians live in Sydney, the city is the epitome of modern-day Australia. Historically, the first penal settlement was founded there; the first confrontations made with the Aboriginal people; the first imprint of a British way of life; the first founding of an agrarian society, with a flock of merino sheep heralding the wealth to come from the 'sheep's back' economy.

Ethnic mix

Until the 1950s, Sydney people were almost totally of British stock. Despite the much-vaunted egalitarianism, there were two distinct classes, represented by the well-established families with 'old money', who could nevertheless be joined instantly by those acquiring new wealth, and the working class, heavily unionized and fighting establishment snobbery. Running through this two-tier social system were the same Irish/English feuds which had been fed to Australian children for four generations.

With the advent of mass immigration from the 1950s onwards, Sydney acquired new blood – mostly Greek, Italian, Yugoslav, Polish, Spanish, Chinese, Lebanese, Indonesian and Filipino. To Sydney's credit, the influx continues to be relatively painless, though Vietnamese boat people are perhaps not as welcome there, any more than they appear to be in the rest of Australia.

Newcomers see it as the 'Lucky Country' and start working at anything in which the entrepreneurial spirit can take them to riches. You will find a Vietnamese selling perfect farm produce at a wayside stall in the country, an Italian taxi-driver, fluent in racing techniques if not in English, or a Chinese computer expert who has fought her way to the top while supporting young brothers and sisters. Ethnic restaurants of superlative quality abound and delicious Lebanese, Indonesian and Italian takeaways are dispensed with smiles from the tiniest of premises. These are absurdly cheap, and they cater for vegetarians.

Sights and entertainment

When you've had enough of the harbour, crossing by ferry to a zoo or to a marvellous seafood restaurant, sailing to the North Heads where the Pacific rollers crash against the sandstone cliffs and the wind blows the spinnakers of a hundred small sailing ships, you can help a river postman deliver mail. Just a short way north of bustling Sydney, people living on the banks of the Hawkesbury River have their mail and supplies delivered to them by mail boat, the last remaining in Australia. Passengers join the mail boat as it winds in and out of sub-tropical fjords, with flashes and screeches of brilliant parrakeets and parrots, and outback families waiting on little jetties.

For contrast, there's Sydney nightlife with flashes and screeches from the colourful Kings Cross area. My favourite Australian fountain is there, the El Alamein, its million jets sparkling in thistledown puffs, drawing people of every nationality thronging the pavements. Parts of the area are sleazy with strip joints and prostitutes and dubious 'entertainment', but it is a curiously colourful mixture, with tourists buying enormous toy kangaroos and didgeridoos amid lots of good-natured banter. It also has its sad side; sometimes a drunken Aboriginal man leaps out into the road to stop cars going by, shouting 'Get off our land! You've no right to be here!' Nobody takes any notice. He's a well-known figure at the Cross, but one is reminded that someone, somewhere, owes him something. Perhaps it is your ordinary Aussie citizens, with their liking for fair play, or perhaps it is the federal government in Canberra, dubbed with typical Aussie humour 'the wise men of the east'.

Ironically, the Aboriginal communities in Sydney and small towns in New South Wales today suffer from too few work opportunities and too much public largesse – their welfare payments give them a higher income than that of poor farmers, and there is little incentive to take advantage of progressive educational policies in the state. With so many other different nationalities being assimilated into the economy, particularly noticeable in New South Wales, there is hope that urban communities can be reconciled.

Outside the capital Sydney is not only the most exciting city in Australia, but also the most convenient from which to see a representative part of New South Wales. The visitor might never wish to leave, with glorious surfing beaches to the north, the Blue Mountains and Canberra all within reach by day trips. Even outback New South Wales, with a visit to a working sheep station, can easily be reached from Sydney. Sheep shearing, with baling and classing of wool, is fun to watch, as are the sheep dog demonstrations. You may remember Paul Hogan climbing over the backs of commuters in a New York subway in *Crocodile Dundee*. He learnt that trick from watching sheep dogs.

Sightseeing

With so much publicity given to Queensland beaches, tourists might not be aware that there are beautiful, uncommercialized beaches in the north of New South Wales, easily reached by a good highway or by train.

Nearer Sydney the Blue Mountains, which really are blue because of an interaction between the lush forests and the mild sun, afford the most wonderful mountain scenery in Australia. People had given up building castles by the time Australia was colonized, but a natural formation of rocks deep in the heart of the largest forest is Australia's only 'Castle'. Then there are the Three Sisters; thin, sharp mounds of rock shooting out of the forest, with a wind-swept path winding around them. You might try the steepest 'railway' in the world – a reckless hurtling from a peak into the forest below, so hold on to your hat.

People who live in small townships in this area tend to be less brash than Sydneysiders, a gentler breed altogether. They commute to the city with difficulty, trains often getting snowbound; Sydney colleagues always assume that late arrivers commute by either the notorious mountain train or the equally infamous Manly ferry (though worse than either, in my opinion, is the terrifying manner in which doors suddenly fly open in a train travelling at speed on the subway).

Information and booking

Tourist information in Sydney about transport, accommodation and places to visit is unequalled in the rest of Australia, not only for the city and the state itself, but for the rest of the country. So if you arrive first in Sydney, plan the rest of your visit from there. But above all, relax and enjoy the harbour city. Many people depart from there only to plan to return as permanent residents.

Australian Capital Territory

In Australia generally, cities became capitals because good harbour facilities made them the centre of trade. Canberra, the national capital, is the exception – chosen as a site because it was the centre of nothing.

At the time of the federation of Australian states, 1901, Sydney and Melbourne were locked in fierce conflict over which city had the greater claim to be the national capital; Sydney even refused to join the federation unless the national capital was in New South Wales. A compromise was reached, acceptable to everybody, but satisfactory to nobody. A national capital would be created, a long way from both Sydney and·Melbourne – 'Out Woop Woop way', as one despairing politician put it. Eleven acrimonious years later, a green area on the slopes of the Great Dividing Range, 320 km southwest of Sydney and 440 km northeast of Melbourne, was designated Australian Capital Territory (ACT).

The following year an American architect, Walter Burley Griffin, won the international competition to design the capital city, Canberra, but the building of it has been an ever-ongoing task because it is essentially an artificial city, founded not on the needs of commerce, but on political necessities. Today 60 per cent of Canberra's inhabitants are employed by government departments, and live in leafy suburbia in an atmosphere rarefied by the high altitude above sea level and an apparent absence of commercial activity.

Australians tell visitors, tongue in cheek, that Canberra is splendidly laid out (as in dead), and weekends see a mass exodus of politicians. In fact, so reluctant were they to go to Canberra in the first place that in 1955 the then prime minister, Robert Menzies, had to order all his government departments to leave

Canberra

Architecture

Melbourne for good. Diplomatic missions were given the same treatment, so reluctantly they, too, left the fleshpots of Melbourne for their new embassies in Canberra. Now a tourist attraction in their own right, the embassies are all built in the traditional style of the country they represent, for all the world like a mini-United Nations sideshow.

There are circular road systems for both the city and the administrative centre, Capital Hill, bisected by the huge artificial lake (called Lake Burley Griffin, naturally), so if you miss something the first time round, just keep on going. My own impression of Canberra is that it is dull, for the most part, with all the action taking place off-stage. However, from the visitor's point of view, it can be seen as one vast exhibition centre, to be enjoyed as a day trip.

War Memorial and Museum

Canberra's Australian War Memorial and Museum attracts more tourists than any other building in Australia except Sydney Opera House. It is a melancholy building, reminiscent of northern France, commemorating the dead of two world wars, the Korean war, and the confrontation between Malaysia and Indonesia. Outside the War Memorial there is an interesting reconstruction of a Japanese midget submarine, made from two which were destroyed in Sydney Harbour in 1942.

By contrast, inside the War Museum is graphically alive, with sound and light models of Australian actions in all the conflicts, and haunting sculptures, paintings, sketches and photographs, all by Australian war artists. There was a terrible loss of life, disproportionate to their small population, in defending the British Empire; but Australians as yet omit to record their earliest battles, fought with Aboriginal people on their own soil.

Other sights

For gentler contemplation, the visitor should relax in the National Gallery and the National Library, both treasure houses not to be hurried through. A Henry Moore bronze reclines by the shore of Lake Burley Griffin, and the vistas are soothing. After seeing the high court, the two parliament houses, and the carillon tower, I formed the distinct impression that I was standing in an architect's model of what a national capital should be, not what life and living had made it.

There is a good city bus tour of 45 km around the lake, which allows the visitor to see the Australian National University, with its enormous astronomical complex, the Royal Australian Mint where the whole minting process is shown, and the Telecommunications Tower. Alternatively, simply take the lake cruise.

Climate

The answer to the child's question of 'Where do the flies go to when they leave here?' is Canberra. In the intense summer heat dark, sticky bush flies settle on faces and arms continually, giving rise to the expression 'the Aussie salute', which is the upraised hand brushing flies away. It is a climate of extremes, with snow-blocked roads in winter, but excellent skiing in the nearby Australian Alps compensates. Many visitors prefer the crisp, cool air of spring, yellow with wattle, and autumn with its blaze of bronze and red.

Officially, one is told that Canberra is the Aboriginal name for meeting place, which seemed an apt name for the national capital. Unfortunately it was later discovered that 'canberry' was a meeting place, and 'canberra' a woman's breasts. Look out for twin hills.

Outside the capital

There is a vast nature reserve, Gudgenby, in the southern part of the ACT, which is an unspoilt terrain of eucalyptus forests, valleys, creeks and craggy mountains alive with birds of every description, shy wallabies and occasionally koalas. You need good walking shoes, a stout heart and preferably a guide.

The local tourist bureau is excellent, and has suggestions and maps in abundance, whether you are there for a day or several weeks. Most Australians would tell you that a day is enough.

Victoria

On the death of Queen Victoria, when the populace shouted, 'The Queen is dead: long live the Queen', they were wiser than they knew. Their monarch was dead, the Victorian era had ended, but the spirit and values of that redoubtable old woman lived on, in a far post of the empire on which the sun has never set – Victoria, Australia, as the Americans say.

Melbourne

Today, the visitor arriving in its capital city, Melbourne, feels the impact of Britishness more strongly than does a visitor arriving in London. The whole city is a monument to the Victorian age – in architecture, in parks and gardens, and in the customs and mores of the people. That Britishness should prevail, when over a million of Melbourne's inhabitants are either recent migrants or first-generation Australians, says a lot for the solid weight of Victorian values inculcated so speedily in the newcomers.

Ethnic mix and Britishness

I was on a train to Brighton (Brighton, Melbourne) one afternoon when hordes of teenagers in various school uniforms crowded in. A schoolgirl with the face of an Italian madonna, though sulky at the time, flounced into the seat beside me. 'They're calling me a Wop', she said angrily 'and they're all mostly Dagoes. Anyway, I was born here, so I'm an Australian. Even my dad's not Italian any more.'

The Melbourne brand of Aussie racism seems funny, rather than offensive. Greeks call Melbourne 'that other Athens', but the indigenous British Melbournians quickly convert them to the conservative practices of the Victorian 'Garden City'. Although more different nationalities have settled in Melbourne than in Sydney, they did not change Melbourne into a cosmopolitan city as they did Sydney; they were simply absorbed into the strong existing culture: public schools (called private schools in Australia – even Prince Charles went to school at Geelong Grammar); rowing on the river Yarra; cricket at the Melbourne Ground, the birthplace of test cricket; horse racing, concerts and opera; and everywhere English parks and gardens and solid middle-class values.

The only thing the immigrants changed was the food. Instead of the roast with three veg or the ubiquitous steak, there are now over 1500 restaurants offering a choice in international cuisine difficult to surpass anywhere in the world. Melbourne claims the A–Z of food – Afghan to Zulu, with everything in between. Melbourne is a gourmet experience, with marvellous wines. The only oddness that strikes the visitor is a curiously defensive attitude, a need for reassurance. A fellow diner will lean across from his table to say: 'Isn't that a good wine? Isn't that the best you've ever had – better than French wine, isn't it?' The remarks are never addressed to the female present (are women still not expected to have an opinion, a taste?) and any conversation must include, from the visitor, extravagant praise of Melbourne food and wine and similarity to all things English. It is as though Melbourne is reluctantly Australian, rather than proudly so, as are entrepreneurial Sydney and those sturdy Aussie outback characters.

For this reason, Melbourne has fallen heavily behind Sydney in the tourist stakes. Melbourne looks back over its shoulder, nervously, and Sydney looks forward, flamboyantly. Anything new in Melbourne, architecturally, is so inhibited by the 'good taste' understatement that instead of producing a Sydney Opera House, it erects an arts centre with a timorous spire barely noticeable by day; a city square with no focal point; a pedestrianized shopping mall ruined by allowing trams to lumber through it.

Sights and entertainment

To enjoy Melbourne, one should live there, not visit. All its pleasures are quiet and intimate, victoriously Victorian. I love the Royal Botanic Gardens with its lakes of wildfowl and flowering trees, overlooked by Government House, a replica of Queen Victoria's holiday home on the Isle of Wight, and Fitzroy Gardens, with its fairy tree and marvellous conservatory filled, when I last saw it, by begonias of such variety and colour it was a memorable Australian experience.

The trams, too, are delightful as well as practical, though if driving in Melbourne there are rules to be observed: trams can be overtaken on the inside lane only, and when the tram stops it is obligatory to stop behind it, because passengers getting on and off the tram take precedence. (In fact, pedestrians are generally well thought of in Melbourne. In the rush hours people pour to and from Flinders Street railway station like thousands of ants fleeing a destroyer, crisscrossing diagonally at intersections. It is the busiest railway station I have ever seen, yet its tourist information service is outstanding, and traffic control allows commuters more than a 'fair go' on the roads.)

One corner of 'Marvellous Melbourne' has become 'Swinging Melbourne'. There is good variety now in entertainment after dark, with concerts, operas, plays, good cabaret acts and alternative theatre, with a festival of comedy. Night-clubs appealing to Young Fogies abound. Some follow the French, and now New York, trend for shared lavatories. Instead of ladies and gents identifying with the famous silhouette, there are 'omnisexual toilets', which should cover all the indecisive varieties. You must travel to the outback to find the real Aussie dunny, a ramshackle wooden structure over a hole in the ground.

Outside the capital   The smallest of all the Australian states, Victoria is also the most populated and the most industrialized. Even in the north, where the Murray River forms the border with New South Wales, international companies are expanding their industrial complexes, particularly around Albury. Small towns between there and Mount Buffalo have made an industry out of tourism, appearing like film sets, rather than places where ordinary people live and work. In towns such as Beechworth each building has been imaginatively restored, making the main street a ribbon development of tourist traps, from tiny museums to arts and crafts centres and antique shops – extremely picturesque, but avaricious. Admire, but drive on to

Mount Beauty in all its free grandeur of greys and
greens in summer and blue-white snow in winter,
with its scarlet parrakeets flying out over the valley.
Bright, the main centre, caters for the summer tourist
and winter skiers very comfortably indeed, at affordable prices.

The only tourist attraction in the whole of Australia   *Phillip Island*
which made me really angry was the much publicized
'Penguin Parade' on Phillip Island, visited from Melbourne. A few scant years ago thousands of fairy
penguins used to waddle out of the sea at dusk, heavy
with fish to disgorge for their young, waiting outside
their burrows in the sand dunes. Now enormous
wooden grandstands have been erected over a wide
expanse of beach, and walkways built over and
around the burrows. There is a nightly spectacle of
horror as these poor creatures, in rapidly decreasing
numbers, are subjected to floodlighting, the roars of
a vast crowd and, despite announcements, camera
flashlights as they try to reach their crying babies
without being blinded. Many are. They stand for-
lornly, heads tucked under a flipper. Not able to
fish again, they and their young starve to death.
Announcements forbidding the use of flash cameras
are made in English only so Japanese tourists
especially are unaware of the danger to the penguins.
Please press the authorities to place prominent signs
with a drawing of a flash attachment and a red bar
across it, because fairy penguins can survive the sea
eagle, but not the tourists.

It is a pity the entrepreneurs behind the Phillip
Island grandstand view of penguin maiming were
ever given a licence when one sees how well other
Victorian tourist attractions can be managed – such
as the Sovereign Hill goldmining area, one of the
best in Australia.

Victoria is so compact that each of the regions can   **History**
be visited quite easily. Historically, they each represent a different stage in the growth of the state.
Whalers and sealers were the first Europeans to arrive
on the southern coast, but built no settlement. An

abortive attempt was made by Sydney to start a colony on Port Phillip Bay in 1803, but the settlers found it dismal and decamped to Tasmania, then called Van Diemen's Land. As the best agricultural land there was gradually taken up, two hardy pioneers decided to return to Port Phillip Bay and try again. So successful were they that several hundred settlers quickly joined them in the area surrounding Melbourne today. In 1837 this *de facto* arrangement was ratified by Sydney, and Melbourne became a thriving community with a grid pattern, if not much else, of the city to be. Even in those days, Melbourne people had a sense of propriety and resented having too many convicts foisted upon them, sending several consignments away.

Landowners and commerce

The pastoralists, having struggled to establish themselves on large tracts of land, quickly became the landed gentry, employing a strange variety of people: ticket-of-leave men (convicts released early for good behaviour), men and women who had served their sentences and Aboriginal people who imparted their bushlore. Supply depots sprang up, and wagons and drays carried the new products from the settlers to trade for the goods they needed – sugar, tea, flour, farm implements, cotton and so on. Commerce flourished and free settlers flowed in, adding their skills to the community. In 1851 Victoria was granted its independence.

Gold mining

Suddenly, however, gold was discovered in New South Wales. The prospect of instant fortune has always been a great lure, and the free settlers followed it. In the Sydney/Melbourne rivalry stakes, Sydney had pulled ahead, but Melbourne was lucky. In a panic search, prospectors found rich seams of gold in Ballarat, not far from Melbourne. It was still 1851, but the new colony had changed irrevocably. People poured into the diggings from the US, Britain and China, and the 'Lucky Country' leapt with its new-found wealth into a golden future. In just five years the Great Australian Gold Rush brought 115,000 people to Victoria and New South Wales.

The miners were called 'diggers', a name proudly carried by Australian soldiers to this day, probably because the original 'diggers' mounted the only rebellion against the crown ever made by Australians. As rebellions go, it was a small one, but bloody. In 1854 a group of diggers barricaded themselves in a wooden structure, the Eureka Stockade, in protest against unfair licensing fees and police harassment. The redcoats were sent in and thirteen minutes later, with fairly indiscriminate shooting, the rebellion was quelled. There were twenty-eight dead, including, as is the way of civil battles, some innocent bystanders. The leader of the rebellion, minus an arm, was spirited away by sympathizers.

By the 1880s, so much gold had been mined in Ballarat and Bendigo that magnificent Victorian buildings, reflecting the great wealth being generated, were built in the gold towns themselves and, of course, in Melbourne. Their solid structures are what makes Melbourne so different from all the other state capitals.

With so much easy money spilling about, Victoria entered a period of lawlessness, and Melbourne, for the only time in its life, was a debauched city. Gangs of bushrangers roamed the countryside, the most notorious being Ned Kelly, who made himself a suit of armour and pitted his horse against government train and telegraph. A much romanticized figure, he was eventually hanged at Melbourne gaol.

After all that excitement, which would not have amused Queen Victoria, Melbourne grew up, and all too quickly became staid.

Sightseeing

When sightseeing in Melbourne and the rest of Victoria, bear its history in mind. You will see very few Aboriginal people, because the original tribes were virtually obliterated, but there is a small nucleus of intelligent, educated Aboriginal people who are seeking to manage their own affairs, in education and social and medical welfare. What you will notice is the wide, and for the most part happy, international mixture of immigrants.

Tours and Unless you are made of money, travel everywhere
excursions by coach. It is worthwhile paying for the half-day
City Sights and Blue Dandenongs tour ($21.50)
because of the variety offered, including all the
important city landmarks. You will have a chance to
see bush country in the Dandenong Ranges, with
wild exotic birds, tree ferns and towering mountain
ash.

Alternatively, an award-winning day tour includes
the Blue Dandenong Ranges, from which you can
then travel by Puffing Billy, the oldest steam railway
operating in Australia, to Menzies Creek. The scenery is magnificent, the train ride exciting. You are
then taken to a winery for wine-tasting and a spit-
roast lunch, and the afternoon ends with the Great
Dividing Range and a visit to an excellent wildlife
park, to see kangaroos, wombats, platypuses, emus
and koalas. Including lunch, the price is $49.50.

For superb coastal scenery, there is a one-day
excursion ($38) which passes Prince Charles's old
school, Geelong Grammar, salt works, a fort, soaring
cliffs and long surf beaches.

Don't go to see the beleaguered fairy penguins on
Phillip Island ($45), but if you're interested in sheep
shearing and sheep dog mustering and trials, there is
a half-day tour to Victoria's Farm Shed, where they
also have a farm animal theatre and you can try to
milk a cow – not as easy as you might think ($22).

There is an interesting three-day excursion to the
Gippsland Lakes and Canberra, then along the Pacific
Coast to Sydney for visitors ($278 including accom-
modation and most meals). I thought a similar three-
day excursion through Mount Gambier to Adelaide
was less interesting for the money ($270) as it doesn't
afford the visitor quite such varied scenery, but it's
still a good package deal.

One of the most popular tours is to Sovereign Hill,
a re-creation of the actual goldfields, where you can
pan for gold and see tents, humpies and mud-brick
huts, as well as going down a mine. Apple orchards,
beautiful botanical gardens at Ballarat and natural
mineral springs at Hepburn give you a good, varied
day ($38).

Bookings are made through tourist offices, hotel or motel reception or travel agents. Tours depart from Flinders Street opposite St Paul's Cathedral, but there are courtesy (free) pick-up points at many hotels, on request.

Information and booking

Tasmania

Local feeling When you travel in Tasmania you may be puzzled to hear local people declaring that they are Tasmanian, not Australian. Emotionally, there is some truth in this, but legally there is not. Tasmania, that huge, shield-shaped island to the south of the continent, is a state in the Commonwealth of Australia. For a long time 'Tassie' grew apples, had a mining boom and a mining bust, and provided temperate holidays for the more urban Australians crossing the Bass Strait. When the urban Aussies returned to Melbourne or Sydney they made what would be racist jokes in other parts of the world, as though Tasmanians were a separate race of mental defectives, all, of course, descended from convicts. It was comforting for mainland Australians to make Tasmanians their scapegoat, but very unfair. Tasmanians retorted that it was the urban Aussies who had a chip on their shoulders about convicts, and what about those ignorant mainlanders who arrived in Tasmania expecting to show their passports and change their currency.

There are, undoubtedly, many Tasmanians who would prefer to hold a Tasmanian, rather than an Australian, passport, and be as separate from Australia as New Zealand is. They, again, are an island people descended from an older island people, without the multicultural leavening so evident in Melbourne or Sydney; but those two cities are not the whole of Australia, whatever their assertions. Rural Australians are similar in whichever state you visit, and Tasmania is not only rural, but wild. Vast areas designated as national parks are not cosy places with flower beds and manicured lawns. In the southwest there is a bushland wilderness, still unexplored, where anything from the Tasmanian tiger to the local equivalent of the Loch Ness monster might lurk.

Tigers and
Devils

Luckily tourists, however macho, could not hope to hack their way through the dense undergrowth in order to claim the government reward for a sighting of the elusive tiger. For the purpose of your holiday, accept that this fierce creature is extinct, at least in those parts of the national parks you visit, and prepare to meet the Devil instead, safely confined. Australia's fiercest animal, the Tasmanian Devil, is untamed even in captivity. The young look deceptively gentle in a zoo, sleeping in a warm huddle like Labrador puppies, while the parents look harmless enough curled in a hollow log, but even the hand that feeds them is not safe. If cornered, they attack people without hesitation, to the death.

History

To me, they symbolize the fierce, cruel history of the country, as did its first European name, Van Diemen's Land, bestowed upon it in 1642 by its discoverer, Abel Tasman, in honour of the governor of the Dutch East Indies. Being Dutch, Tasman could not have foreseen the evil connotation to British ears, a century and a half later, of a 'Demon's' land, with or without the Van. Tasman was merely passing by on his way to 'discovering' the existence of New Zealand, but the name hung over the island like the wicked fairy's christening present, not to be banished before an entire race of Aboriginal people had been destroyed, and members of the colonizing race brutalized beyond even the savage custom of the time. Eventually the wicked fairy's gift was returned to sender, and in 1856 the by now infamous colony was renamed Tasmania. The 'demons' vanished, the transportation of convicts ended, and a great influx of free settlers struggled to establish for lawless Tasmania a new identity, the acceptable face of British respectability.

Remnants of convict settlement, when it was Van Diemen's Land, have been conserved, rather than obliterated, so one is more conscious of its historical significance in the founding of present-day Australia in Tasmania than one is in the other states.

European settlement   Because of fears of French colonization, the island was formally claimed for Britain in 1802, and the following year the first settlement was made at Risdon, near what is now the capital, Hobart. The year after, for strategic reasons, another was made in the north, soon moved to the site of Launceston today.

If you visit the west coast and take a 30 km cruise of great beauty from Macquarie Harbour and along the Gordon River, you will see Sarah Island, where the first penal settlement was made. It is the setting for the most interesting book to have been written about life in a convict settlement and the inhumane treatment of prisoners who were shipped from England to the new colony. One of the greatest of Australian classics, historically accurate, it is a novel by Marcus Clarke – *For the Term of his Natural Life* – almost unbearable in the reading because it tells of such unnatural lives of endless torture, starvation and hopelessness.

Perhaps the most notorious penal settlement was that of Port Arthur, on the Tasman Peninsula not far from Hobart. It was a natural choice, being easily guarded by a chain of vicious dogs across a narrow neck of land and shark-infested waters. A few convicts did escape and joined Aboriginal people, only to be hunted down later.

Port Arthur   Port Arthur provided the severest form of punishment for prisoners too difficult to contain in Sydney, as well as taking convicts transported directly from England, who ran the full gamut of scurvy, floggings, torture, treadmills and heavy chains. There was a separate prison for boys, some as young as ten, exported as part of England's 'criminal class', as severe as their extreme youth could stand. In time, the penal settlement became self-sufficient, producing coal and sawn timber, cut stone and leather goods as well as food. Stone buildings were erected in place of wooden structures, the settlement supporting at its peak 1000 free people, including the garrison officials and their families, as well as 1200 convicts.

After the end of transportation of convicts from England, Port Arthur remained a prison settlement for twenty years. An elderly population of ex-convicts, still relatively sane, were housed as free paupers, but an asylum was necessary as the last major construction at Port Arthur for 111 'lunatics', aged forty to sixty, many of whom had been rendered mad by the cruelties at the prison on distant Norfolk Island.

It is difficult to comprehend the degree of sadism condoned by the British government, when even the so-called model prison, designed originally by a more spiritual mind to reform prisoners through contemplation and solitary work, became the worst place for recalcitrant prisoners to be sent, because of the insidious brainwashing techniques employed. Prisoners did 'solitary' in total silence, the warders communicating by hand signals and wearing felt slippers to avoid sound. Prisoners at chapel and in silent exercise yards were compelled to wear head-masks, thus obliterating any trace of identity remaining after their names had been taken away – depersonalized to a number.

In the end, convicts and their warders were ferried a short distance to share the same accommodation in the Isle of the Dead. The convicts, however, leave no tombstones to bear witness to their 1769 dead, their anonymity following them into mass graves. During the same period 150 of the free population died there, with eloquent tombstones to speak of natural hazards.

In Tasmania today there are many gracious Georgian buildings constructed by convict labour, but at Port Arthur you will see, fittingly enough, only ruins. A chill wind blows from the Antarctic, but there is a more sombre chill of suffering to be sensed in that area of 'demons'' land. I would advise you not to linger among the ruins, but to head for the open road.

Travel and accommodation

Although tourism in Tasmania lags behind that of the other states, that has its advantages as well, when you consider what those busy little builders have perpetrated in 'developing' the southern coast of Queensland. Travelling by car around the island can be a joy, giving you the freedom of exploration so vital to your full enjoyment of this state, which coach tours do not. There are inland lakes and mountains, nineteenth-century stone villages and scenic coastal routes, not simply to be flashed past, but to linger over. You can picnic on a deserted beach with a smooth granite boulder for a table, gather shells of intricate beauty and watch the seas surging through blow-holes. All the natural delights are there in abundance; but not, alas, many restaurants or petrol stations to help you enjoy them. In tiny fishing ports you will see fish being gutted and crayfish despatched – but not unfortunately being cooked.

When exploring by car it is wise, therefore, to set off from a large town with a full tank of petrol, water and emergency food supplies. For the European traveller, used to finding accommodation for the night in any place that takes your fancy, there are shocks. Remember Tasmania is sparsely populated, and accommodation not found by chance. Public telephones on a highway are something of a rarity, and givers of tourist information much slower than on the mainland, so you need a battery of coins to establish where you might find a bed for the night. It is safer to visit a large tourist information centre in person and book your accommodation for four or five nights ahead, according to which region you expect to be in.

Accommodation   Accommodation ranges from five-star hotels in major towns to a tent on camping grounds in national parks, with no services whatsoever. Host farms, Colonial accommodation (see 'Getting in and out of beds: accommodation') and fishing and hunting lodges are perhaps the most interesting, but also the most variable. If you insist on having your own bathroom, it is wiser to stick to large hotels and motels in cities, using them as your centre for day trips; but if you can stand a few surprises, both pleasant and unpleasant, the other possibilities are most rewarding. Spend time studying the particulars. Colonial accommodation in a large town, for instance, might offer neither old-world charm nor modern comfort, but Colonial accommodation in a rural area may be quite different – Campania House near Richmond, for example, set in a hundred acres of farmland, offers warm and friendly hospitality in one of the oldest houses in Tasmania built by convict labour.

Road signs are not good in rural areas, so if you want to avoid the pub regulars all arguing over the best way past where Charlie used to live, mark the location on your touring map and get signposting details from your host when you ring to book. Remember also to arrange for an evening meal with them if you wish, generally better than eating in a small town restaurant.

Agriculture is still recovering from the loss of its export market when the UK joined the EEC, so host farms are glad to welcome and even entertain you, a marvellous boon if you are travelling with children. It is interesting to see their way of life if you are a country lover, and a welcome change from the anonymity of motels.

Motels Some forty years ago, the first motel in Australia was built in Tasmania, at Eaglehawk Neck, to cope with the influx of mainland Australians curious to see the old penal settlement at Port Arthur. Motels generally, whether part of a chain or independently run, are reliable, and occasionally luxurious. Some offer comprehensive holidays at very reasonable prices.

Hotels Be guided by your price range for hotels, but the smaller ones can be a bit on the sleepy side for service, and are as yet unborn in many parts of the country. They are, however, at least a twinkle in the eye of the government, now keen to attract international travellers. A series of lodges is planned for the wilderness areas, and two large, new five-star Sheraton Hotels will open shortly in Hobart and Launceston, which no doubt persuaded Qantas to include Hobart as an international destination.

Casino-hotels There are several casino-hotel complexes, the most famous being West Point in Hobart, where, as well as every type of gaming for avid Australian gamblers, there is excellent accommodation and sophisticated cabaret entertainment.

Each year the Sydney-to-Hobart yacht race generates enormous excitement, and New Year's Eve in Hobart with the victors celebrating in the streets has a great, infectious gaiety.

Touring Tourism is just behind mining and forestry in producing revenue, so take advantage of the extraordinary range of choice you are offered as a tourist, and don't be afraid to go off the beaten track. Escorted wilderness tours, both walking or by off-road vehicles, lasting from one to fourteen days, lead you into a world of giant ferns, a horizontal forest and ancient gum trees, streams, lakes and waterfalls. Wooden huts with fireplaces give a rustic rest, deeper than most town dwellers could imagine. Resist the temptation to go off bush walking on your own without contacting a national park ranger first, because it could be dangerous. Going only a little way into the bush from a track can be very disorientating, and in a short time the newcomer is hopelessly lost, or as Aussies say 'up a gum tree', only too literally meaning 'looking for bearings'.

Explore as much as possible, but play safe by having overnight accommodation to aim for. We set off merrily one afternoon from Devonport, planning to drive across the central mountains and spend the night at a hotel on the western shore of the Great Lake, dining on fresh trout. My mistake lay in thinking an unsealed road meant a reasonable sort of dirt road, not sharp rocks. At a low speed because of puncture risks, for hour after hour there was no sign of life except a few uninhabited wooden holiday shacks, with no prospect of sizzling trout. Had I known then that one of the shacks belonged to the prime minister of Australia, and that his telephone set among the trees was solar powered, I might have been more confident of arriving somewhere, anywhere, before dawn; but suddenly the promised land appeared – lights, habitation, a barking dog. More of a hunting lodge than a hotel, the Compleat

Angler was magic. A blazing log fire flanked by antlered deer heads, a genial host and excellent food and wine sprang to life, with fascinating stories spilling from the deerhunters and fishermen.

Everyday can be an adventure if you are open to new impressions and prepared to make your own itinerary. Ask for help if you need it. Life is lived at a slow pace there, so relax and go with it. Their seafood, trevally and crayfish, is amongst the world's best, and the scenery magnificent and unspoilt. There are wild populations of brown trout and rainbow trout in most of the lakes and streams, and deer in the forests, so trophy hunters will be in their element.

Simply because the wildlife is so prolific in Tasmania there is great carnage on the roads caused by careless motorists. If driving fast at night, it is difficult to avoid kangaroos, wallabies, wombats and occasionally the ever-rarer koala. They are all nocturnal animals who become hypnotized by lights, and often cannot escape in time because so much more land is becoming fenced. I hope you will see these gentle creatures in wildlife parks, not under your wheels. *Risks to avoid*

Visitors should also be aware of the risk of bush fires. Cigarettes and matches should always be extinguished before discarding. Camp fires, including barbecue appliances, should have surrounding dry grass cleared in a radius of 3 m before lighting, should never be left unattended and should be completely extinguished before leaving. Sometimes there is a day of total fire ban in the open air, while throughout the year no fires must be lit in areas of peat, sand dunes or marram grass.

Although there is a danger of bush fires in Tasmania just as there is on the mainland, you never have to battle against enervating heat and humidity there. The climate has four seasons, as in Britain, with a similarly uncertain summer, so instead of sun barrier creams always pack one really warm jumper and a wind- and rain-proof jacket. In winter (July–August) there is skiing in the national parks, but away from the mountains snowfalls are rare. Spring is perhaps **Climate and clothing** the most beautiful time, with waves of daffodils and blossom and the midland paddocks full of new lambs.

The people   The farmlands, with their rolling hills and hedgerows, are generally greenly reminiscent of the English countryside, but when I was last there, in March 1988, drought had scorched and burnt the land to the colours of the outback in mainland Australia. No resemblance to England remained except in the architecture of old villages and farmhouses and the nature of the people.

Apart from the city dwellers of Hobart, Launceston and Devonport, the rural areas seem to have encapsulated an England of an earlier time, where people seem reserved, suspicious of strangers and often poorly educated. Some have never travelled far from their own part of the country, and eke a meagre living from the land. Small communities are scattered over a vast area, ill served by public transport, so that old customs are perpetuated. There are 'landed gentry' who live in beautiful old colonial houses and ensure their children are well educated, while some poorer country folk in isolated pockets think a little writing and arithmetic, of necessity by correspondence, sufficient for their children as it was for them. The rich, evidenced by the yachting fraternity, appear to be very rich, and the poor, as on isolated small-holdings, very poor and inarticulate.

You might meet eccentric characters such as the woman deerhunter who had seen no life outside her native forest; a drover, moving sheep on agistment (from one part of the country to another for better pasture), who would never sleep under a roof; or a man I couldn't wait to escape from, so full of sly innuendo, exhibiting macabre exhibits in his tiny museum. But there are also accomplished, unusual people, such as two entrepreneurs, one with an excellent working steam-mill and the other, knowledgeable and informative about wildlife, with an imaginative, well-managed zoo, or such as the very able chief executive of Abel Tasman, who has done so much to make the sea-way to Tasmania a wonderful experience.

Of all the states in Australia, almost to my surprise, I found Tasmania to be one of the most rewarding for the tourist, because it is not based on a single city, but is an enormous area of great variety, totally unspoilt by either manufacturing industry or tourism. Take a chairlift over a foaming gorge, a cruise on a fishing boat, put on your walking shoes or drive through crisp, delightful days in a climate more temperate than the rest of Australia's. Tasmania may be the smallest state in the Commonwealth, but it is one of the most enjoyable.

Northern Territory

To travel in the Northern Territory is to travel back in time: there are few monuments to humanity. Instead of looking at the tallest building in the world, or the largest Disneyland, you are seeing and understanding 'as it was in the beginning'. There are so many species of bird and beast, such riotous colour in lagoons of water lilies, in mighty gorges cloven in red and in the changing light at sunset. It is here that you know why the land is sacred to the Aboriginal people. There is a spiritual peace in certain places stronger than I have felt in a cathedral.

Prehistory and history The very heart of Australia, that ancient red centre dominated by Ayers Rock, was once a great inland sea. Because the continent is the oldest in the world, one can only imagine what leviathans were beached

'*Take your hat off, Fred. According to this we're standing in St Paul's Cathedral.*'

(Reproduced by kind permission of Douglas E. Tainsh)

when new land erupted and the sea drained dry.
There is, however, one astonishing survivor from
that period, in the most unlikely place for a sea
creature – the summit of Ayers Rock.

After a heavy rainfall, pools on the summit fill
quickly, and renew life in a species of crustacean, the
shield shrimp, which originated in that inland sea
150 million years ago. Like flower seeds in the desert,
the eggs of the shrimps lie dormant until there is
enough water to renew their life cycle. But if you
think the little shield shrimps on the top of Ayers
Rock had ancient beginnings, they were latecomers
compared to the Rock itself, which geologists believe
was part of a mountain range thrust out of the seas
500 million years ago.

During the Ice Age, northern Australia had land
bridges to New Guinea and possibly to the Asian
continent. As the ice melted and the sea levels rose,
islands to the north of Australia were still far nearer
than Tasmania, or even the southern mainland. For
this reason, the Top End of the Northern Territory
had Asian influences before European, and today
Darwin is a multicultural city with an Asian/Aborigi-
nal slant, rather than European.

The first British settlement in the Top End, Port   *Macassan*
Essington, was not made until 1838, but for centuries   *trade*
before that proas from the central Indonesian port of
Macassar, with their great triangular sails made of
matting, had voyaged regularly to 'Marege', the name
they gave to Australia. In the shallow bays round
Arnhem Land, on the western coast near Darwin,
and off its islands, the Macassans sought a curious
sea-creature which was smoked and exported as far
as the rich markets of China and Japan. Generally
known as trepang, it is a kind of sea slug, or sea
cucumber, believed in Asia to be the ginseng of the
sea, a man-root endowed with aphrodisiac properties. Be that as it may, the Macassans certainly interbred with Aboriginal women, often having to fight
for them, and the trepang-eating Chinese and
Japanese had a big population increase.

Trepang-processing plants with smoke-houses and
huge tubs frequently employed Aboriginal labour

and Aborigines sailed to Macassar on the proas. There are interesting cave paintings of proas and muskets, and evidence that various skills and products were exchanged, the least fortunate being the introduction of alcohol to the Aborigines.

European exploration and settlement

The harbour at Darwin was 'discovered' in 1839 by a British ship carrying the scientist Charles Darwin, while the first European land exploration of the Northern Territory was made by Ludwig Leichard, who set off from Brisbane in 1844. Fourteen months later, minus three of the party who had been speared by Aboriginal people along the way, they reached Port Essington, near Darwin. It was a journey of 4800 km through desert and wetlands, forests and canyons, living off the land.

In the 1880s there were several year-long, epic, pioneer journeys made by settlers moving cattle from Adelaide to the Katherine region south of Darwin, and even from Queensland, to take up squatters' rights on vast holdings.

Gold mining

The population did not increase noticeably, however, until the discovery of gold brought many nationalities to Pine Creek (between Darwin and Katherine), leading naturally to settlement and development in the Top End. Subsequently, Darwin became unique in Australia, perhaps the forerunner of a more Eurasian country, where Asian, European and Aboriginal cultures merged harmoniously. At the Top End, skins vary from palest gold to black, children especially reflecting many admixtures of race.

Coping with destruction

In 1942 Darwin had reason to regret its proximity to Asia when it was repeatedly bombed by the Japanese, but even greater devastation was caused naturally in 1974, when Cyclone Tracey flattened most of Darwin during one terrible night. It was Christmas Eve when the cyclone struck. It started off badly enough, with families huddled together in the parents' double bed, then cowering underneath it, and finally all pressed into their shower unit, the strongest internal structure.

One poor mother, the last one crawling from underneath the double bed, was sucked out through a tumbling wall as the roof careered off. Next morning – Christmas Day – she was found, wounded but alive, beneath debris in a neighbour's garden. She owed her life to being sheltered by her stout kitchen cooker and refrigerator which had been blown out with her. 'Only natural they saved me', she said laconically, 'I'd slaved over that cooker for years.' A phlegmatic attitude to cyclone, drought or flood is typical of people in the Northern Territory. After all, nature is bigger than they are.

Races, treks and flights

'Down the track' from Darwin is Alice Springs, once a staging post in the overland telegraph line from Adelaide to Darwin, selected because it was near a permanent water-hole. Locals in 'The Alice', giving you directions, say 'It's over the river'; the bemused tourist sees a bridge, but alas no water. It's all part of an outback joke. The River Todd is permanently dry, so the Henley-on-Todd Regatta, held annually in August, has more boat races than Henley in England, but not on water. The boats have no bottoms and the hull is held at waist level, so there are hilarious sights of many hairy legs, like a boated caterpillar, racing down the dry, sandy course.

Somewhat faster are the camel races in May, but tourists on a camel safari are taken at a steadier pace through some of the more inaccessible places in the red centre. One of the safari brochures invites you to 'take your camel to dinner', which simply means that the camel will be a rather novel taxi for a comparatively short journey. Riding a camel is not too arduous, but you need to be reasonably fit. This applies to hot air ballooning as well. If you can't squat and hold onto the rope handles in the wicker basket, don't attempt it – but the dawn flights are breathtaking.

Many tourists consider it obligatory to fly to central Australia to see Ayers Rock, climb it, and then fly away as soon as possible to Darwin or Cairns. Aborigines think they're mad. The most photographed geographical feature in Australia, Ayers

Rock is best enjoyed not by climbing it or flying round it, but by gazing at it, from sunrise to sunset. The changing lights and colours are the Rock's fascination. There have been a few fatal heart attacks to unfit tourists climbing it, so be warned.

The people   Only 1 per cent – 140,000 – of Australia's population live in the Northern Territory, and nearly half of this number is in Darwin. Full statehood has not been achieved yet, but there are mutterings of an organized withholding of taxes until they get full representation. At present the federal government controls Aboriginal affairs, national parks and uranium mining. All of these are vexed questions for the local people, exacerbated by the American Communications Centre at Pine Gap, near Alice Springs. As they point out, it makes them a prime target for attack.

The most fiercely independent of Australian people, Territorians will probably be granted full statehood soon. There is nothing genteel here, or British, as in Victoria, Tasmania and Queensland. If you travel in luxury within the Territory, you will see some of the great wonders, comfortably, from the base of a five-star hotel, but will miss the people. A pity, because they are as rugged and colourful as the country itself.

In the Top End, I asked a motel manageress if she could possibly persuade the air-conditioning unit in our room to activate itself. She didn't want to activate anything – 'It's my weight you see', she said as she patted the tent-like garment enfolding her, 'but it's great in the sea. I floated for forty-eight hours once.' Despite her girth, she had apparently spent several happy years working as the only female deck-hand on a fishing/prawning vessel in the Timor Sea. During heavy seas she was swept overboard. Although it was dark and no-one on board had witnessed this, there was no panic. Her Asian mother had taught her how to remain suspended in the sea effortlessly, and her Aboriginal father had assured her that she would not die in water. So rather like a large inflatable doll she simply crossed her arms behind her head, and floated until the fishing vessel found her forty-eight hours later. 'I didn't mind', she said, 'because I kept my fags and lighter watertight in my pocket, so I just smoked and had a sleep. I knew they'd come back for me. I was a bloody good deckhand.'

She was not such a good manageress – we left before our air-conditioning was mended – but in temperatures of 35 °C and above, no-one moves quickly in the Northern Territory unless a crocodile is slithering down a nearby bank.

Because of the vastness of the area, there are two distinct climates; the monsoonal Top End and the desert centre, both posing problems for the unwary visitor flying in from a temperate zone. The best months for travel are from May to October.

Climate

The Top End has two seasons, the wet from November to March, and the dry from May to September, tailing off gradually. During the wet, temperatures in Darwin soar to 40 °C, and the humidity is very trying. Despite a torrential downpour, I discarded a raincoat, preferring the warm rain to my own stickiness. The winter season, the dry, has temperatures in the low 30s, sometimes lower, when Darwinians don a woollen jumper in the mornings. In the dry season, wildlife is concentrated dramatically into smaller areas as rivers, lagoons and billabongs contract, making tours of the wetlands very exciting.

The Top End

Don't get carried away by either your excitement or a crocodile. There are gruesome stories of tourists being seized while swimming in rivers, and even one of a hapless American woman who leant out of a touring launch to wash her hands and was suddenly wrenched from the boat before anyone could save her. Her head was found among the mangroves forty-eight hours later. Crocodiles drown their victims and take them off to secret lairs until the decomposing bodies become succulent.

There is also danger in the sea, from November to March, when the box jellyfish, a lethal stinger, claims several lives each season. Some locals say it is safe to swim in a wet suit or with the limbs covered by nylon stockings which prevent the tentacles gripping, but I suddenly found swimming pools more attractive.

The desert centre   'Down the track' from Darwin there are no threats from water – indeed the threat is from a lack of it. In the centre, it is generally dry. The summer season, from October to May, has peak temperatures of over 40 °C. In December and January there is no humidity, but dehydration is a danger. When every living thing crawls off to find shade, only mad dogs and tourists go out in the midday sun. One youth who wandered from his party without carrying water was found dead in less than twenty-four hours. At the other end of this heat scale tourists, though warned, are shocked to find the temperature at night falling to below freezing point during July and August, wintertime in the centre. The days, however, are still hot, and the sun is directly overhead all the year round. Though there is no wet season and the annual rainfall is very low, there are fierce rainstorms intermittently throughout the year.

Clothing   With these extremes of climate to contend with, make sure you have suitable clothing. For the Top End, jeans, good walking shoes, a hat, insect repellent and sunscreen are essential for both seasons, and an umbrella or raincoat for the wet. If camping, a mosquito net is your best friend. For the centre, jeans or shorts and a loose cotton shirt, good walking shoes (not sandals or trainers), a hat, a water container and sunscreen; if there in July and August, add a track suit and thick jumper, while campers need very warm sleeping bags.

Sightseeing   There are so many package tours available, with excellent guides, that it's not worth going it alone, as you would in Tasmania. Because of the distances involved, air flights are advisable to at least one of the centres, where accommodation ranges from the luxurious to the tent. After that, choose a coach, a four-wheel drive, a camel, a balloon or of course your feet. Each of the national parks has a different character, matched by that of your guides.

On Melville Island an Aboriginal tribe, the Tiwis, accept tourists from May to October in a safari camp just half an hour's flight from Darwin. This is tourism on their terms, with visitors joining in hunting expeditions for turtle eggs and crabs, bush creatures or mussels from the mangroves. Conventional Aussie fare, rather than bush tucker, is provided for visitors, but you can at least catch your own fish.

Aboriginal sites

   Care should be taken to comply with strict national park regulations for your safety as well as for the protection of the environment. Kakadu, to me the most beautiful part of Australia, is very well managed, the Aboriginal people allowing access to sacred sites in return for a share in the profits from tourism and mining. In return, visitors are asked to avoid damage to ancient rock paintings by not rubbing against them; not to bring firearms, traps and nets into the park; to light fires only in the fireplaces provided; to keep dogs on a leash at all times; and not to damage or remove flora and fauna.

For your safety, it is recommended not to drive at night. In the Top End there are buffaloes, and 'down the track' there are wild camels, horses, kangaroos and other wildlife, any one of which can mean a serious accident. All coaches and four-wheel drive vehicles are fitted with metal grids to deflect bodies hurtling towards the windscreen, so be warned.

Driving

When boating, carry safety equipment and extra fuel in tidal areas. A combination of shifting sand and mudbanks can leave your boat stranded in places where huge and watchful crocodiles guard their young. Their camouflage is so effective, blending with the colours of water, mud and logs, that you might think it safe to leave the boat to push it off the banks. Don't. Two evil, hungry eyes are probably watching, so stay in the boat and wait for help or for the tide to turn.

Boating

If all these warnings have alarmed you into thinking the Northern Territory is a place to avoid, I'm sorry. With care, and preferably with guided tours, you will enjoy every day of this ancient world. Explore the unexpectedness of a lagoon which beckons like an English meadow, green and speckled with tiny lotus blooms, and vast escarpments where Aboriginal people lived for some 40,000 years, painting and hunting, telling stories and singing songs in praise of the living land.

South Australia

Visitors to Australia are naturally drawn to charismatic images such as Sydney Harbour, the Great Barrier Reef, Ayers Rock or Kakadu National Park. South Australia can boast no such natural wonder; but South Australia does boast a moral wonder. In a country where a penal colony was the reason for founding every other state, South Australia is the only one founded by free settlers.

History

Oddly enough, the progenitor of this idea of attracting British gentry to buy tracts of land was himself in prison in England at the time, serving a three-year sentence for abducting an heiress. Upon release, he set up a colonization society which fired so much enthusiasm that the British government reluctantly implemented the plans of the ex-prisoner; the South Australia Foundation Act was passed, and a governor, free settlers and their livestock arrived in the new colony in time for Christmas 1836.

South Australia was to be, in every way, a model colony. Aboriginal people were to be given equal rights with Europeans, and a protector of Aborigines was appointed. Land was sold at approximately $1 per acre, and settlers fanned out along the coast and onto Kangaroo Island. As Aboriginal people had no concept of landownership, there were inevitably clashes when they not only continued their traditional hunting over 'settled' land, but added mutton to their bush tucker. There were many complaints from settlers, who soon took reprisals, but on the whole far less bloodshed occurred in South Australia than in the other colonies.

Adelaide

South Australia was also fortunate in having an enlightened surveyor-general, who designed the site of Adelaide with such a vision of the future that today it is still a model of town planning. The city centre, laid out on a grid pattern, is completely surrounded by a green belt a kilometre wide, and beyond the northern residential area a sweeping arc of hills, the Mount Lofty range, frames the outer limits.

As befits Adelaide's founding vision, it is the most gracious, elegant city in Australia, originally built entirely of stone. Apart from some unsympathetic glass blocks, the dignity from the past remains.

Character The architectural dignity is mirrored in the character of the people. South Australians are proud of their lineage. Sydney is concerned with how much money you have; Melbourne asks which school you attended; Adelaide enquires about your ancestry. It has always been called the city of churches. The original proclamation urged sobriety and worship upon the free settlers, and this they observed faithfully, looking with disdain upon the convict origins of their neighbouring states. Naturally enough, other Aussies called Adelaide people 'wowsers', the ultimate epithet Down Under for a killjoy. Nevertheless, the first legal nudist beach appeared near Adelaide, and a 'street of shame' slunk into being in the city centre. Suffice it to say that poor old much-maligned Hindley Street has a long way to go before it catches up with the lures of traditional red-light districts.

Adelaide people are very well behaved, reserved and quiet, the only women on view in the peaceful evenings being engrossed in beauty treatments in the countless beauty parlours – more than there are restaurants – abounding. I was astonished by the evening trade, clearly visible through shop fronts, of facials and manicures. But that was Glenelg, a delightful seaside suburb, reached by a marvellous old tram from the centre. A day there ends with happy, sandy people boarding the old brown tram with fish and chips and draught champagne.

Wine Wine is very much a feature of Adelaide's life. Australia's now famous wine industry began in South Australia, when Lutherans left religious persecution in Prussia and Silesia in the 1840s to settle in the Barossa Valley, a short drive from Adelaide. About a quarter of all Australian wine is produced there, and the happy tourist has a choice of forty wineries to sip amongst, with the German influence still strong enough to produce a lot of wassailing during vintage festivals, held in odd-numbered years for four days in March–April.

In the even-numbered years, Adelaide holds its famous arts festival in the festival centre from February to March. Visually the centre does not compare with Sydney Opera House, but functionally it is excellent, with a complex of auditoriums and theatres attracting some of the most diverse and innovative work in Australia as well as stars from overseas. It stands elegantly amid gardens and lawns sloping to the River Torrens. In fact the Torrens is not so much a river as a dam, and the water is pumped out and replaced regularly, but the swans accept it with the usual gracious Adelaide charm.

Arts festival

Speaking of water, the stuff comes out of taps in Adelaide a most disconcerting shade of pale yellow. The early settlers blamed the Aborigines for urinating in the river, but whatever the excuse now offered, I drank the bottled variety. Still, the drinking water is not a real hazard, and there are no crocodiles in the Murray River if you wish to explore it by paddleboat – only human sharks operating the boats. This is a leisurely way of seeing the countryside, either as a day trip or for a week – very relaxing, but rather expensive, I thought.

River and sea

Seabathing is sedate but delightful, in water that is less salty than on the Pacific eastern coast of Australia, and tiny glittering fish swim with you in a friendly way. On Kangaroo Island, where whalers established a base before South Australia was colonized, seals sunbathe on the southern coast, lifting their great snouts to the blue skies. Surfing beaches are not as crowded as in Queensland, but have the same fine silver sand, and long breakers.

To me, Adelaide is the most peaceful of Australian cities, with a warm, temperate climate which encouraged Mediterranean settlers to plant groves of olive trees, now wild and rampant in the foothills. Curiously enough, to the north and west there is a larger stretch of desert than in any of the other states, without any permanent water. Originally camels and their Afghan cameleers were brought in to carry supplies 'up the track', and helped in the building of the railways and the overland telegraph. In World War I there was an Australian Camel Corps which covered itself in as much glory as the Light Horse, but camels on the whole are not well regarded. A South Australian bushman who pioneered camel trekking for tourists in the 1970s is doing much to dispel that image. He claims that people suffering from stress, bad backs or simply too much contact with cities are healed in every way by camel trekking in remote country – 'They get so laid back', he said, 'you can pick up the pieces and hang them in the trees.'

Less relaxing are some of the coach tours in the Adelaide hills, not to be visited on a rainy day: 'Behind the mist is a fairy-tale castle you can't see . . .' When a passenger asked if the road was dangerous, the driver shrugged and said, 'If anyone is frightened of going up steep hills, just close your eyes; I always do.'

Some of the picturesque towns such as Hahndorf, visited by all the coach tours, are designed as tourist traps, and should be treated accordingly, but 960 km from Adelaide in the desert outback is the most extraordinary town in Australia, Coober Pedy. The Aboriginal meaning of the name is 'white man's hole in the ground', but even this could not prepare you for the barren, rocky moonscape. 'If this is a town, where is it?' asked a small boy. Across the ridged and pitted land nothing moves. The temperature was 40 °C, and the sun cruel. But underground the rocks were honeycombed with dwellings, and the air was cool. Beds were carved from the rocks; the walls were rock; there was even a ballroom of sorts. Often extravagantly furnished, these warrens of coolness are the homes of the Coober Pedy miners, real outback characters who would not live anywhere else. Their life is extracting opals, those shimmering, pale stones which radiate every colour in nature.

Whenever I am in the outback I hear what is almost a singing of the light. Travel, if you can, to the Flinders Range, now a national park, where light falls in purples and ochres, and bush wallabies come to drink at sunset, while the wedge-tailed eagle rests on the warm air.

Travel

South Australia is not the most tourist-minded of the states, but to my mind is all the better for that. If you arrive in Adelaide by plane, the airport has free phones to accommodation listed and photographed, with plenty of vacancies except during the arts festival. If driving, observe notices about petrol stations before embarking 'up the track' on the Stuart Highway, and don't attempt the outback on your own. If arriving by train on the famous Overland from Melbourne, you will be amply rewarded. The mood and atmosphere of the countryside is a far cry from the cities of the eastern seaboard. Trees are lonely figures and a town appears like a ghostly illusion, shrouded in mist. Through the Adelaide hills dawn brings lit cowsheds and Friesians waiting to be milked. The whole panorama of Adelaide lies below, a city built of stone, founded by proud people.

You will not arrive at the famous railway station in the city. That is now an international casino. (Its marble halls were used for the ballroom scene in Cairo in the film *Gallipoli*.) It is worth visiting, even if you don't gamble, to see what epitomizes the vision of that surveyor-general, William Light, who built a fair city.

Western Australia

Queenslanders are known as banana benders; on the other side of the continent, Western Australians are called sandgropers – the difference being that people from Western Australia don't mind their epithet. They are the least hung-up, the most assured of Australians, and after all, there is a lot of sand in the state; vast deserts and a coastline of such forbidding barrenness that for centuries explorers were too appalled to lay claim to it. Only 'naked savages' could live there, chasing strange creatures which carried their young in pouches.

Perth and Fremantle

In the capital, Perth, the sandgropers are laughing. In a multimillion aura, with the fastest growing economy in Australia, they can afford to. Perth's super-rich carry mining profits in their pouches, and bound about in yachts and jets. Over a million people live in Perth, leaving a scant 400,000 to scatter themselves very thinly over the rest of Western Australia – one third of the continent's landmass, its area is that of western Europe from the Arctic to the Mediterranean.

In 1696, a Dutch explorer landed on an island near Fremantle and discovered it was swarming with small, grey, furry creatures. Horrified, he named it Rottnest (Rats' nest) Island and escaped as from the plague. Today that island is an enchanting holiday place, and the tiny marsupials, quokkas, are loved by tourists for their friendliness and charm. A few kilometres away on the mainland, the people of Perth seem to have emulated the quokkas. They, too, congregate in the small southwest corner, and are noted for their friendliness and charm. You will hear a lot of British accents in Perth, because the ideal climate and lifestyle attract many British immigrants; clear skies of an intense blue, even temperatures and sunny days, with a glorious city, good housing and beaches, boats and river, and bushland for a city park.

Ordinary people are proud, not resentful, of their *The good life* multimillionaires because the good life is there for everyone to enjoy, greatly enhanced by entrepreneurial investment of the right kind. Before the summer of 1986–7, when the America's Cup yachting trophy was to be retained, or lost, in the fierce winds off Fremantle, that southwest corner smartened itself up for the world audience. Architectural eyesores were demolished; buildings of historic interest were restored; new hotels, shopping malls and restaurants arose to complement the high-rise buildings by the river, and thousands of trees were planted. As a result, Perth and Fremantle are second only to Sydney in a harmony of land and water, people and lifestyle. There is a good ethnic mix, most immigrants being assimilated with ease, and Perth is confident of its future.

Sailing and the turf are obsessions, with enormous amounts of money backing them both ways. The horses enjoy a lifestyle unrivalled by most people. At two magnificent studs near the capital there are private training tracks, plunge pools and green paddocks by the river. While there is a general bonhomie exuded by the sporting entrepreneurs, they are reputed to be 'as tough as goats' knees'. Be that as it may, they won the America's Cup after 112 years of American domination, and when they lost it, they lost gracefully.

Founded in 1829 by a group of mainly ex-army and **History** navy settlers, the new colony fought for its existence against fierce Aboriginal people. In 1848, after a severe crop failure, the settlers appealed to Sydney for help, not expecting a consignment of almost 10, 000 convicts. Much alarmed (and outnumbered by two to one), the settlers next turned to the British government, who obligingly despatched 5000 men and women, free settlers all, as reinforcement.

Mineral wealth

For fifty years, progress was slow, until, as in Victoria and New South Wales, gold was discovered – at Kalgoorlie, 550 kilometres east of Perth – leading to a gold rush which populated and developed the state. There is a statue of the discoverer, an Irish prospector called Paddy Hannan, pouring water from his canvas water bag in perpetuity, but the fountain symbolizes more than water in that thirsty sand. His discovery of gold led to a rush for mineral wealth which has never abated in Western Australia. As well as gold, silver, lead and zinc are mined throughout the state, while in the Kimberleys there is an embarrassment of diamonds and in the Pilbara region there is iron ore in superabundance. Oil and natural gas have been discovered off the northwest coast and uranium is known to be in the north.

Potentially, Western Australia could be the largest mine in the world, artificial craters, canyons and mountains replacing those formed in the continent's last upheaval. Mining is a vexed question. On Aboriginal reserves it is forbidden by statute, but large international companies still operate there. Most of the mineral wealth is in the northern part of the state, a long way removed from the government in Perth. People in the Kimberley region would prefer to be governed from Darwin, because their links are there, not in the far-removed southwest corner, but the potential riches from that area are too great for Perth ever to allow the northern part of Western Australia to join the Northern Territory.

Broome

Being nearer Jakarta than Perth, the coastal region of the Kimberleys had the same Asian beginnings in settlement as did the Top End of the Northern Territory. Broome was once the world's pearling centre, and today is a colourful mixture of predominantly Asian races, Japanese, Chinese, Malaysian and Filipino, who interbred with Aboriginal and white Australians. As in Darwin, there is no racial tension. There is an ease of life which attracts many young Australians to live there on unemployment benefits, surfing and fishing.

In August there is the Festival of the Pearl, Shinju Matsuri. This began more than a century ago when hundreds of pearling luggers celebrated the mother-of-pearl, the oyster, and that elusive little irritant which grew inside it – the pearl. The size of the Japanese cemetery testifies to the dangers the divers faced, and Chinatown today allows you to imagine the flavour of what was an Asiatic port.

If you drive to Broome from Port Headland across the Great Sandy Desert, you might be thirsty enough to join in the drinking marathons at the Roebuck Bay Hotel, but it's difficult to tell who are the aggressors, the chuckers-out or the chucked. The streets are sandy and pot-holed, unlit from the airport, but you know when you're in Broome by the corrugated iron roofs and names like Fong's, Yuen Wing, Tong's Cafe, Mango Jack's and Wackett Aircraft. Only the Broome tourist office looks new.

Remote areas

No wonder Perth is known as 'the most remote capital in the western world'. Most Australians on the east coast visit Europe or Hawaii or Bali, rather than Western Australia. Oddly enough, even Perth people simply don't travel in their own state. The roads north are marked by 'wayside daisies' of 'tinnies' – discarded beer cans; and the roadhouses along the way are apt to measure distances as 'six tinnies up the track'. The road trains (very long container lorries) do the coastal route regularly, but even for four-wheel drives, much of the interior is inaccessible.

The nearest one Perth couple I met had been to the deserts of wild flowers was walking through their city's conservatory and gardens, and yet in the southwest every spring there is a breathtaking spectacle of variegated flowers in colours as exotic as parrots' plumage, filling the forest floor and endless plains.

Wave Rock and desert

A little further north, near Hyden, there is the most extraordinary sculpture I have ever seen, surpassing anything a human has chiselled – the Wave Rock, curved and crested, poised three times above human height, threatening to crash on a sea's edge for over two billion years. As the Opera House has become Sydney's symbol, the Wave Rock, to me, is the natural symbol of Western Australia. Perth is pretty, but the ruggedness of rock formations and the endless silence of the desert is a natural wonder. You can trace in the sand the small prints of the thorny devil and darting dragons, tiny descendants from the time when great dinosaurs roamed, perhaps in forests bordering an inland sea. In the Pilbara region, great gorges cut the Hamersley Range in reds and ochres, purples and grey-greens, and silver waterfalls into dark, cool pools.

It is country where you can know yourself, find or lose yourself, or even die. The lure of space and distant horizons can be dangerous to anyone not born in the region. Recently two young stationhands died in the scorching heat of the desert in the northwest. Now all jackeroos, as the trainee station managers are called, will join new training schemes in survival skills in outback Western Australia. The tourist, not so trained, should never go off the beaten track without a guide.

The Hutt River Province

You will be surprised to hear of an independent principality near Geraldton, the Hutt River Province, formed when 'Prince Leonard of Hutt' seceded from Australia. The self-styled ruler issues his own passports and stamps, and appears to be tolerated by Canberra. Don't think it's like Monaco, and be tempted to visit. It's a rather droll tourist trap, because its attractions are nil, but it saves the entrepreneur from working too hard on an arid station.

Tourism

The deserts have largely been formed because of a cold ocean stream, the west wind drift, which flows from the Antarctic north along the West Australian coast, so even in summer the sea is cold. This is offset, to a certain extent, by the constant warm sunshine, and in the southwest many people are hardy enough to swim or surf all the year round, sunbathing and picnicking in the sand dunes. However, tourists should be wary, as the locals are, of the dunes from September to October, because the venomous dugite snake, always prevalent in the area, begins to become active at that time.

Tourism in Western Australia is still very new, and outside the southwest corner life can be as rugged as the landscape. Roads are long, hot and dry. As one roadhouse owner said, 'It's not for the moaner mouths. Sink another tinnie and cool off.' Before you dive into the sea, however, ask the locals if it's safe. There is a shallow bay at Monkey Mia, near the most westerly town in Australia and carefully watched by wardens, where you can sport with dolphins, delighted as puppies to have someone to play with. There is an ancient Mediterranean belief that dolphins evolved from the same root as man, and their musical voices and laughing mouths would make me, for one, want to claim them as clowning cousins. Elsewhere in the area sharks are prevalent, while at Port Headland you are warned about sea snakes, octopuses and stonefish. April to September is the best time to visit, as after that cyclones can strike at any time.

Tours of the Kimberley region are better organized from Darwin than from Perth (remember to avoid the wet season from October to March). Perhaps the most spectacular scenery in the whole of Australia lies in the Kimberley area, the last frontier of a 'settled' land. It was called the Never-Never, and enjoyed a romantic image of remoteness and innocence until June 1987, when five people enjoying camping holidays were suddenly murdered in the most bizarre way. A crazy hunter flew from Germany to play a macabre game with his victims. They had been fishing on remote rivers, the Victoria and the Pentecost, when they were seized, and their cars set on fire. Naked, they were set off to flee wildly through the bush until he hunted them down and shot them. An enormous man-hunt was mounted from Kununurra by police from both Western Australia and the Northern Territory, using telephone links through the Royal Flying Doctor Service to far-flung cattle stations in the North, and Aboriginal trackers. The killer was caught at Fitzroy Crossing.

Curiously enough, the Fitzroy River is home to the harmless Johnston crocodile, with which you can swim safely. Personally, I prefer dolphins.

The Southern Cross

I did not find gentleness
under that harsh sun
and left as outlaws do
driven outside the dry earth
of Australian birth.

My face lifted to love
in soft rain and old cities,
high steepled to a Gothic cry,
a European many times before.

But not that only: not only that.
In that dark space between the stars
where hangs the Southern Cross
I saw my footprints fixed
before the feet were formed.
In that dark space between the stars
there swings a silent pendulum
which marks the time our world can live,
with all our little lives to come and go.

From Dreamtime's cradle came the Man,
totemic Ancestors calling up the land
in sacred song, each gully, rock and billabong
a flurry of feathers, fur and fins –
such births and baptisms in the Beginning
as sunsets of cockatoos flew
through the waratah's bushfire flowers
into a blue jacarandah blooming.
Red the big Man Kangaroo,
red the dust he springs above,
warm the fur of big man Roo
who seeds the pouch I bounded from.
Mooloolabah, Maroochydore,
thudding surf and ocean swell

within the shell, without the shell.
You called them all, you called them well.

When you consider how the land was loved –
ten thousand years of walkabout
in footprints reverent to earth,
with nothing pillaged, nothing raped,
the Aborigine is perfect global man,
whose worth
we may not understand
until Antarctica melts to one great wave.
Australia . . . . . . Australia.

Eleanor Greet

Useful addresses

State tourist offices

Australian Capital Territory
Canberra Tourist Bureau
Jolimont Centre
Northbourne Avenue
Canberra City ACT 2601
Tel. 062–45 6464

New South Wales
Travel Centre of NSW
16 Spring Street
Sydney NSW 2000
Tel. 02–231 4444

Northern Territory
Northern Territory Government Tourist Bureau
31 Smith Street
The Mall
Darwin NT 5794
Tel. 089–81 6611

Queensland
Queensland Government Travel Centre
196 Adelaide Street
Cnr Adelaide & Edward Streets
Brisbane QLD 4001
Tel. 07–226 5337

South Australia
South Australia Government Travel Centre
18 King William Street
Adelaide
Tel. 08–212 1644

Tasmania
Tasmanian Tourist Bureau
32 King William Street
Adelaide SA 5001
Tel. 08–211 7411

Victorian Tourism Commission
230 Collins Street
Melbourne VIC 3000
Tel. 03–619 9444

Victoria

Holiday WA Centre
772 Hay Street
Perth WA 6000
Tel. 09–322 2999

*Western
Australia*

Airlines

Oxford Square
Cnr Oxford & Riley Streets
Sydney
Tel. 02–268 1111 (reservations)

*Ansett Travel
Centres*

Cnr Hunter & Phillip Streets
Sydney
Tel. 02–693 3333 (reservations)

*Australian
Airlines
Travel Centre*

Australian Home Accommodation
Suite 4, 209 Toorak Road
South Yarra Victoria 3141
Tel. 03–241 3694

**Youth
hostels**

Australian National YHA Office
60 Mary Street
Surrey Hills NSW 2010
Tel. 02–212 1512 5844

Farm Holidays
PO Box 384
Woolahra NSW 2025
Tel. 02–387 6681

Farm stay

Host Farms Association
7 Abbott Street
North Balwyn
Victoria 3104
Tel. 03–857 6767

Getting lost: Index

Aborigines 9, 48, 51, 56, 57, 65–9, 73, 113, 115, 126–7
accommodation 17–22, 99–103, 112
  backpackers 21
  camping 21, 75
  colonial accommodation 19
  farm stays 20–1
  hotels and motels 17–19, 100–2
  house exchange 22
  station holidays 76, 83
  youth hostels 21, 75
Adelaide 18, 48, 49, 115–18
Alice Springs 19, 26, 109–10
America's Cup 121
art galleries 48
Ayers Rock 19, 106, 109–10

Ballarat 98
banks 30
Barossa Valley 40
Barrier Reef 19, 21, 24, 33, 36, 38, 46, 49, 58, 71, 74, 76
Bass Strait 96
Bendigo 93
birds 55, 58
Blue Mountains 83
box jelly fish 76, 111
Brisbane 72–5
bush tucker 53, 56, 71–2
bushrangers 93

Cairns 22, 26, 27, 46, 54, 58, 74–5
camels 109, 113, 118
Canberra 85–7
Cape York Peninsula 21, 76
casinos 46, 49
chemists 34
Coober Pedy 118
crocodiles 54, 76, 111, 113, 125
currency 30–1
Cyclone Tracey 108

Daintree 71
Darwin 19, 48, 108–13, 125
diggers see gold rush
Dreamtime 65, 126

echidna 51
Eureka Stockade 93

films 47
Flying Dctor 72, 125
Fremantle 120
fumigation 23, 59–60

Gold Coast 17, 19, 46, 74–5
gold rush 92–3
Grand Prix see Adelaide

Hamilton Island 17, 75
health insurance 33
Henley-on-Todd 109
Hobart 36, 98, 101–2, 104
honour system 19
Hunter Valley 40
Hutt River Province 124

immigration 9, 60, 62, 73
  control of 23
  mode of entry 10–13
  policy 19
  what to take 10–13
Indian pacific 26

jackeroo 5, 124

Kakadu 18, 58, 113
Kalgoorlie 122
kangaroos and wallabies 52, 57
Kimberly 122, 125
koalas 53, 57, 62

lung fish 51

Macassans 107
measurements 33
Melbourne 37, 48, 49, 88–95
Melville Island 113
mining 108, 122
Mount Isa 71
museums 48
music and dance 46–8

nuggets 31

penal settlement 72, 81, 92, 98–9
Perth 19, 26, 120–5
platypus 51, 58
Port Arthur 98–9

quokkas 120

rain forests 57, 58
recipes 42–4
reptiles 54
Rudall River 67–9

school of the air 72
Seven Mile Beach 36

sport 45–7
Stockman's Hall of Fame 72
Sydney 48, 80–4

transport
    coach 26–7, 29
    flights 25, 112
    hot air ballooning 109
    NSW 83–4
    NT 112–13
    Q'LD 74–7
    rail 25–6
    TAS 99–102
    VIC 94–5
    water 28–9, 113
Tasmanian Devil 57, 96–7
Tasmanian Tiger 96–7
telephones 31–2
television 48
times 3
theatre 47
Top End 107–13
Townsville 22, 27, 46, 58, 74–5

Wave rock 123

Getting found: Map

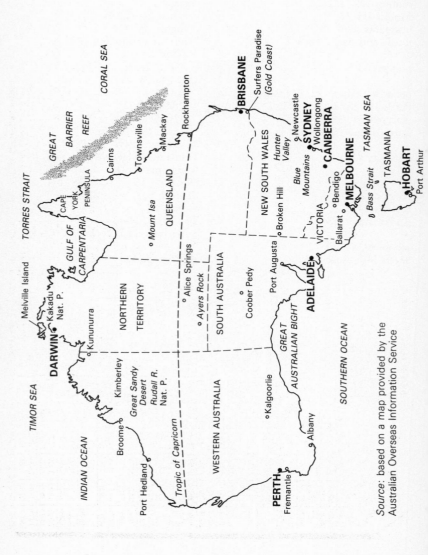

Source: based on a map provided by the
Australian Overseas Information Service

Table of road distances in miles and kilometres.

The roman figure in the square where the horizontal and vertical columns meet is the road distance in **kilometres** between two towns.

The figure in italics shows the road distance in **miles** between the two towns.

* Road distance to Hobart exclude the Melbourne-Devonport ferry journey.

Source: Australian Tourist Commission

Each cell shows **kilometres / *miles***.

	Adelaide	Albany	Alice Springs	Ayers Rock	Brisbane	Broken Hill	Cairns	Canberra	Darwin	Hobart*	Kununurra	Mackay	Melbourne	Mount Isa	Perth	Port Hedland	Surfers Paradise (Gold Coast)
Albany	2675 / *1662*																
Alice Springs	1555 / *966*	3594 / *2233*															
Ayers Rock	1597 / *992*	3636 / *2259*	446 / *277*														
Brisbane	1992 / *1238*	4269 / *2653*	3026 / *1880*	3472 / *2157*													
Broken Hill	513 / *319*	2790 / *1734*	1670 / *1038*	1712 / *1064*	1479 / *919*												
Cairns	2858 / *1776*	5135 / *3191*	2307 / *1434*	2753 / *1711*	1710 / *1063*	2345 / *1457*											
Canberra	1230 / *764*	3905 / *2426*	2785 / *1731*	2827 / *1757*	1315 / *817*	1100 / *684*	2938 / *1826*										
Darwin	3261 / *2026*	3735 / *2321*	1706 / *1060*	2152 / *1337*	3672 / *2282*	3376 / *2098*	2953 / *1835*	4233 / *2630*									
Hobart*	999 / *621*	3674 / *2281*	2554 / *1587*	2596 / *1613*	1970 / *1224*	1113 / *692*	3291 / *2045*	903 / *561*	4260 / *2647*								
Kununurra	3248 / *2018*	3735 / *2321*	1693 / *1052*	2139 / *1329*	3659 / *2274*	3363 / *2090*	2940 / *1827*	4400 / *2734*	880 / *547*	4247 / *2639*							
Mackay	2100 / *1305*	4377 / *2720*	2391 / *1486*	2837 / *1763*	1718 / *1068*	1783 / *1108*	700 / *435*	2325 / *1445*	3037 / *1887*	2971 / *1846*	3024 / *1879*						
Melbourne	747 / *464*	3422 / *2126*	2302 / *1430*	2344 / *1456*	1847 / *1148*	2105 / *1308*	3039 / *1888*	651 / *405*	4008 / *2490*	252 / *157*	3995 / *2482*	2719 / *1690*					
Mount Isa	2734 / *1699*	4773 / *2966*	1179 / *733*	1625 / *1010*			1128 / *701*	2724 / *1693*	1825 / *1134*	3070 / *1908*	1812 / *1126*	1212 / *753*	2818 / *1751*				
Perth	2720 / *1690*	409 / *254*	3639 / *2261*	3681 / *2287*	4314 / *2681*	2835 / *1762*	5180 / *3219*	5646 / *3508*	4206 / *2613*	3719 / *2311*	3326 / *2067*	4422 / *2748*	3467 / *2154*	3442 / *2139*			
Port Hedland	3847 / *2390*	2105 / *1308*	3289 / *2044*	3737 / *2322*	5289 / *3286*	4531 / *2815*			2510 / *1560*	5338 / *3317*	1630 / *1013*	3654 / *2270*	5286 / *3285*	1927 / *1197*	1696 / *1054*		
Surfers Paradise (Gold Coast)	2028 / *1260*	4305 / *2675*	3106 / *1930*	3552 / *2207*	80 / *50*	1559 / *969*	1790 / *1112*	1235 / *767*	3752 / *2331*	2074 / *1289*	3739 / *2323*	1090 / *677*	1822 / *1132*	2396 / *1489*	4393 / *2730*	5369 / *3336*	
Sydney	1475 / *917*	3791 / *2356*	2831 / *1759*	2873 / *1785*	1031 / *641*	1161 / *721*	2636 / *1638*	302 / *188*	4095 / *2545*	1141 / *709*	4096 / *2545*	2061 / *1281*	889 / *552*	2061 / *1281*	3996 / *2483*	5692 / *3537*	933 / *580*